gnuplot Cookbook

Over 80 recipes to visually explore the full range of features
of the world's preeminent open source graphing system

Lee Phillips

[PACKT] open source
PUBLISHING   community experience distilled

BIRMINGHAM - MUMBAI

gnuplot Cookbook

First published: February 2012

Production Reference: 1170212

Published by Packt Publishing Ltd.
Livery Place
35 Livery Street
Birmingham B3 2PB, UK..

ISBN 978-1-84951-724-9

www.packtpub.com

Cover Image by Aaron Grove (aaron@blowfishstudios.com)

Credits

Author

Lee Phillips

Reviewers

Andreas Bernauer

David Millán Escrivá

Acquisition Editor

Usha Iyer

Lead Technical Editor

Dayan Hyames

Technical Editors

Sonali Tharwani

Vishal D'souza

Copy Editor

Laxmi Subramanian

Project Coordinator

Kushal Bhardwaj

Proofreader

Joanna McMahon

Indexers

Tejal Daruwale

Hemangini Bari

Production Coordinator

Melwyn D'sa

Cover Work

Melwyn D'sa

About the Author

Lee Phillips grew up on the 17th floor of a public housing project on the Lower East Side of Manhattan. He attended Stuyvesant High School and Hampshire College, where he studied Physics, Mathematics, and Music. He received a Ph.D. in 1987 from Dartmouth in theoretical and computational physics for research in fluid dynamics. After completing postdoctoral work in plasma physics, Dr. Phillips was hired by the Naval Research Laboratory in Washington, DC, where he worked on various problems, including the NIKE laser fusion project. Dr. Phillips is now the Chief Scientist of the Alogus Research Corporation, which conducts research in the physical sciences and provides technology assessment for investors.

I am grateful to the users of my gnuplot web pages for their interest, questions, and suggestions over the years, and to my family for their patience and support.

About the Reviewers

Andreas Bernauer is a Software Engineer at Active Group in Germany. He graduated at Eberhard Karls Universität Tübingen, Germany, with a Degree in Bioinformatics and received a Master of Science degree in Genetics from the University of Connecticut, USA. In 2011, he earned a doctorate in Computer Engineering from Eberhard Karls Universität Tübingen.

Andreas has more than 10 years of professional experience in software engineering. He implemented the server-side scripting engine in the scheme-based SUnet web server, hosted the Learning-Classifier-System workshops in Tübingen. He has been the reviewer for numerous scientific articles, research proposals, and books, and has been a judge in the German Federal Competition in Computer Science on several occasions. His main interests are functional programming and machine-learning algorithms.

David Millán Escrivá was 8 years old when he wrote his first program on 8086 PC with Basic language. He has more than 10 years of experience in IT. He has worked on computer vision, computer graphics, and pattern recognition. Currently he is working on different projects about computer vision and AR.

I would like to thank Izanskun and my daughter Eider.

www.PacktPub.com

Support files, eBooks, discount offers, and more

You might want to visit www.PacktPub.com for support files and downloads related to your book.

Did you know that Packt offers eBook versions of every book published, with PDF and ePub files available? You can upgrade to the eBook version at www.PacktPub.com and as a print book customer, you are entitled to a discount on the eBook copy. Get in touch with us at service@packtpub.com for more details.

At www.PacktPub.com, you can also read a collection of free technical articles, sign up for a range of free newsletters and receive exclusive discounts and offers on Packt books and eBooks.

http://PacktLib.PacktPub.com

Do you need instant solutions to your IT questions? PacktLib is Packt's online digital book library. Here, you can access, read and search across Packt's entire library of books.

Why Subscribe?

- ▸ Fully searchable across every book published by Packt
- ▸ Copy and paste, print and bookmark content
- ▸ On demand and accessible via web browser

Free Access for Packt account holders

If you have an account with Packt at www.PacktPub.com, you can use this to access PacktLib today and view nine entirely free books. Simply use your login credentials for immediate access.

Table of Contents

Preface

Why gnuplot?

gnuplot is a free, open source plotting program that has been in wide use since 1986. It's used as the graphics backend by many other programs, so plenty of people use gnuplot without knowing it. If you've used Octave, Maxima, statist, gretl, or the Emacs graphing calculator, you've already used gnuplot.

gnuplot was originally designed to visualize scientific data, but its use has expanded to encompass every domain where sophisticated and accurate plotting is required. gnuplot is used in science, engineering, sociology, mapping, business, finance, and computer systems and network monitoring.

gnuplot excels at complex 3D graphing with hidden-line removal and at the rendering of surfaces and contours. It can produce almost any type of graph imaginable (except for pie-charts—but it can be convinced to do this, too, as we'll show later!) for a dizzying array of output devices, and can save plots in almost any type of common file format (and some uncommon ones). It can be installed on any type of computer system you are likely to encounter; there are binaries available for Windows and the sources can be compiled on most reasonably modern machines. I have compiled the latest version (4.4) of gnuplot on both Linux and Macintosh (OS X) computers and verified that all of its advanced features are fully available on both of these architectures. The recipes in this book that illustrate features newly appearing in version 4.4 are marked with [new].

gnuplot can easily be automated. It has its own scripting language and can be controlled from many general-purpose programming languages. gnuplot can also be incorporated into various publishing and document creation workflows to help create professional books, papers, and online documents.

Why this book?

Because of gnuplot's many years of deployment and sophisticated community of expert users, help is usually easy to find in some form. If you are trying to solve a tricky plotting problem, there is a reasonable chance that someone online has either figured it out or is willing to share some ideas about how it might be done.

However, there is little available in the form of a convenient reference with the structure of a cookbook, where you can look for an example of the type of plot you are trying to create and see instantly how it can be done, with a runnable example.

This book is designed to be that combination of reference and tutorial. It goes beyond plotting recipes, however, and will show you how to incorporate your graphs into documents, how to create interactivity, how to program and automate gnuplot, and more. Each example is in the form of a recipe with immediately runnable code in electronic form, and with clear explanations that will show you how to modify the recipe to solve your particular problem. Each recipe is illustrated with the plot created by the procedure, so you can use the book as a visual index that will allow you to quickly find the solution you are looking for.

One of our goals is to show you the major new features in the latest release version of gnuplot, version 4.4.3. Even experienced users of gnuplot are likely to find these sections useful, as we include an illustrative recipe for each new feature; these are specially marked so that features making their first appearance in gnuplot 4.4 can be located quickly. These new features include the use of Unicode characters, transparency, new graph positioning commands, plotting objects, internationalization, circle plots, interactive HTML5 canvas plotting, iteration in scripts, lua/tikz/LaTeX integration, cairo and SVG terminal drivers, and volatile data.

What this book covers

Chapter 1, Plotting Curves, Boxes, Points, and more, covers the basic usage of Gnuplot: how to make all kinds of 2D plots for statistics, modeling, finance, science, and more.

Chapter 2, Annotating with Labels and Legends, explains how to add labels, arrows, and mathematical text to our plots.

Chapter 3, Applying Colors and Styles, covers the basics of colors and styles in gnuplot, plus transparency, and plotting with points and objects.

Chapter 4, Controlling Your Tics, will show you how to get your tic marks and labels just right, along with gnuplot's new internationalization features.

Chapter 5, Combining Multiple Plots, shows how to arrange a set of graphs on the page, and make inset plots.

Chapter 6, Including Plots in Documents, delves into incorporating your plots into technical documents, presentations, and web pages.

Chapter 7, Programming gnuplot and dealing with data, covers how to use gnuplot's built-in programming constructs as well as its ability to be used from any programming language, and how to use the new volatile data features.

Chapter 8, The Third Dimension, shows how to plot surfaces, vectors, heat maps, and lines in a 3D space.

Chapter 9, Using and Making Graphical User Interfaces, introduces several GUIs for gnuplot and includes writing a web application with gnuplot on the backend.

Chapter 10, Surveying Special Topics, covers several special techniques and applications: mapping; labeled contours; colored and broken axes; pictures; and more.

Appendix, Finding help and information, provides a brief list of sources of gnuplot information and education.

What you need for this book

The prerequisites for this book are that you have an installation of gnuplot available for your use and that you are familiar with elementary gnuplot operation (starting gnuplot on the command line and entering a plot command). You should be able to create plots on one of the screen terminals and to save a plot file, as well. Other than that, no specialized knowledge is required to make use of this guide; although we may take examples from various specialized fields, they are incidental to the recipes, which are focused on creating particular types of graphs. The examples of controlling gnuplot from programming languages use simple examples that can be understood even if you don't have experience with the languages used in the recipes.

Who this book is for

Whether you are an old hand at gnuplot or have just started using it, this book is a convenient visual reference that covers the full range of gnuplot's capabilities, including its latest features. This volume is ideal for the gnuplot user who needs complete, runnable scripts to solve specialized graphing problems and clear explanations that will allow him or her to immediately modify them for the tasks at hand.

Conventions

In this book, you will find a number of styles of text that distinguish between different kinds of information. Here are some examples of these styles, and an explanation of their meaning.

Code words in text are shown as follows: "To make a file with data that forms a parabola flipped upside down, tell gnuplot to `set table 'parabola.text'`"

A block of code is set as follows:

```
set y2tics -100, 10
set ytics nomirror
plot sin(1/x) axis x1y1,100*cos(x) axis x1y2
```

When we wish to draw your attention to a particular part of a code block, the relevant lines or items are set in bold:

```
set samples 1000
set parametric
plot sin(7*t), cos(11*t) notitle
```

Any command-line input or output is written as follows:

```
plot 'randomnormal.text' volatile
```

New terms and **important words** are shown in bold. Words that you see on the screen, in menus or dialog boxes for example, appear in the text like this: "We clicked on the tab **Add plot commands** to get the window."

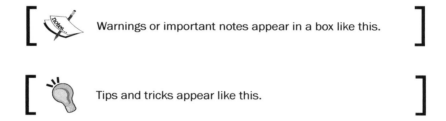

Warnings or important notes appear in a box like this.

Tips and tricks appear like this.

Reader feedback

Feedback from our readers is always welcome. Let us know what you think about this book—what you liked or may have disliked. Reader feedback is important for us to develop titles that you really get the most out of.

To send us general feedback, simply send an e-mail to feedback@packtpub.com, and mention the book title through the subject of your message.

If there is a topic that you have expertise in and you are interested in either writing or contributing to a book, see our author guide on www.packtpub.com/authors.

Customer support

Now that you are the proud owner of a Packt book, we have a number of things to help you to get the most from your purchase.

Downloading the example code

You can download the example code files for all Packt books you have purchased from your account at `http://www.packtpub.com`. If you purchased this book elsewhere, you can visit `http://www.packtpub.com/support` and register to have the files e-mailed directly to you.

Errata

Although we have taken every care to ensure the accuracy of our content, mistakes do happen. If you find a mistake in one of our books—maybe a mistake in the text or the code—we would be grateful if you would report this to us. By doing so, you can save other readers from frustration and help us improve subsequent versions of this book. If you find any errata, please report them by visiting `http://www.packtpub.com/support`, selecting your book, clicking on the **errata submission form** link, and entering the details of your errata. Once your errata are verified, your submission will be accepted and the errata will be uploaded to our website, or added to any list of existing errata, under the Errata section of that title.

Piracy

Piracy of copyright material on the Internet is an ongoing problem across all media. At Packt, we take the protection of our copyright and licenses very seriously. If you come across any illegal copies of our works, in any form, on the Internet, please provide us with the location address or website name immediately so that we can pursue a remedy.

Please contact us at `copyright@packtpub.com` with a link to the suspected pirated material.

We appreciate your help in protecting our authors, and our ability to bring you valuable content.

Questions

You can contact us at `questions@packtpub.com` if you are having a problem with any aspect of the book, and we will do our best to address it.

1
Plotting Curves, Boxes, Points, and more

This chapter contains the following recipes:

Introduction

We begin the book with a set of recipes that cover gnuplot's one-dimensional graph styles. A 1D graph refers to the plotting of data or mathematical functions where the values plotted depend on a single variable. Examples are simple mathematical functions, such as y = sin(x), or 1D data, such as the temperature in a particular location versus time. The plotting of quantities that depend on two variables is covered starting in *Chapter 8, The Third Dimension*, where we show how to make surface, contour, and image plots.

Gnuplot can create a vast array of 1D plot types in a large number of styles. The recipes in this chapter survey all of the major types of 1D graph, with an example that can be run immediately to produce the result in the illustration. For each example, we have provided enough explanation in the *There's more...* section for you to extend and adapt the recipe for your particular problem. We assume that you have gnuplot up and running and are able to create plots on one of the terminals; the recipes in this chapter work on every terminal or output file type.

Plotting a function

gnuplot can be used as a tool to interactively explore the structure of mathematical functions, as well as to create illustrations for publication or education. It has built-in knowledge of both elementary functions, such as sine and cosine, and some special functions, such as Bessel functions and elliptic integrals. The following figure shows the plotting of the besj0(x) function:

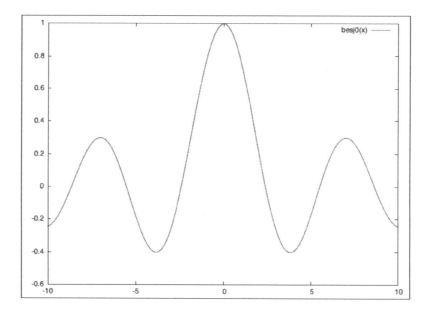

Getting ready

Start up an interactive gnuplot session and make sure that your graphic terminal of choice is selected, and working, using the `set term` command (for example, at the console you simply type `gnuplot`, and, to change the default terminal to X Windows, type `set term x11`).

How to do it...

Type `plot besj0(x)` at the console. The plot in the figure should pop up immediately.

There's more...

Gnuplot understands a big handful of mathematical functions, listed in Section 13.1 of the official manual (the official gnuplot documentation can be found at gnuplot's home, `http://gnuplot.info/`). It also understands all the basic mathematical operators, with a syntax similar to Fortran or C, so you can combine functions into expressions, as shown in the following command:

```
plot [-5:5] (sin(1/x) - cos(x))*erfc(x)
```

In the previous command, we have also shown how to use the [a:b] notation to limit the plot to a specified range on the x-axis.

Plotting multiple curves

You will often want to plot more than one curve on a single graph, all sharing the same axes. This is simple in gnuplot: just separate the functions or datafiles by commas, and gnuplot will plot them in a sequence of colors or curve styles, with a legend so you can identify them. The following figure shows the plotting of multiple curves:

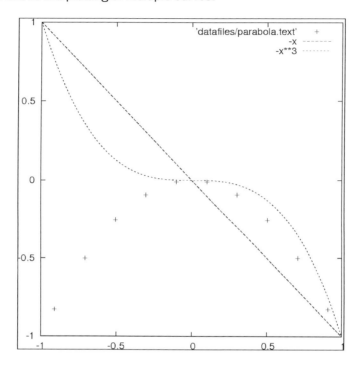

Getting ready

It will be useful to have some datafiles on your disk for use with some of the plotting recipes. You could make them by hand with a text editor or write a program in your favorite language to generate them, but gnuplot can do this itself. To make a file with data that forms a parabola flipped upside down, tell gnuplot to `set table 'parabola.text'`. Make sure to include the quotes around the filename. Then say `plot -x**2`. This writes a table out to the file `parabola.text` rather than making a picture. Now, say `unset table`. You should have a file called `parabola.text` in the directory in which you started gnuplot. Keep it around so we can use it later.

How to do it...

After setting your terminal back to the graphics device you want to use at the gnuplot console, type the following command:

```
plot [-1:1] 'parabola.text', -x, -x**3
```

How it works...

Gnuplot plots the curves using three different colors, dash styles, or line thicknesses, depending on the terminal in use, with a legend so you can tell them apart. The functions are plotted as smooth curves, as we did earlier, and the data from the file is plotted as a series of points, by default; one for each point in the range. This can all be adjusted, as we shall see in *Chapter 3*, *Applying Colors and Styles*.

Take a look at the datafile that gnuplot created to see the format it understands. After several comment lines beginning with the "#" character, we find a series of x coordinates and y values. The last character on each of these lines is a letter: "i" if the point is in the active range, "o" if it is out of range, or "u" if it is undefined.

Using two different y-axes

Sometimes our curves can or should not share the same *y*-axis. Gnuplot handles this with its **tics** commands, which we cover in greater detail in *Chapter 4*, *Controlling your Tics*. The following figure is a plot of two functions covering very different ranges; if the two curves were plotted against the same *y*-axis, one would be too small to see:

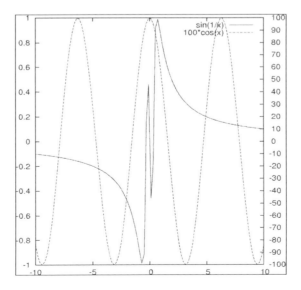

How to do it...

The following simple three-line script will create the previous figure:

```
set y2tics -100, 10
set ytics nomirror
plot sin(1/x) axis x1y1,100*cos(x) axis x1y2
```

 You can download the example code files for all Packt books you have purchased from your account at http://www.packtpub.com. If you purchased this book elsewhere, you can visit http://www.packtpub.com/support and register to have the files e-mailed directly to you.

How it works...

Gnuplot can have two different *y*-axes and two different *x*-axes. In order to define a second *y*-axis, use the y2tics command; the first parameter is the starting value at the bottom of the graph, and the second is the interval between tics on the axis. The command set ytics nomirror tells gnuplot to use a different axis on the right-hand side, rather than simply mirroring the left-hand *y*-axis. The final plot command is similar to the ones we've seen before, with the addition of the "axis" commands; these tell gnuplot which set of axes to use for which curve.

There's more...

One of our functions, sin(1/x), oscillates infinitely quickly near x = 0. Experiment with issuing the command set samples N before the plot command to see how more information is plotted near the singularity at the origin if you use larger values of N.

You can have two *x*-axes as well (but be careful, this can often lead to plots that are difficult to understand). The following script is used to set the ranges of the two *x* axes to be different:

```
set x2tics -20 2
set xtics nomirror
set xrange [-10:10]
set x2range [-20:0]
plot sin(1/x) axis x1y1, 100*cos(x-1) axis x2y2
```

The previous script creates a plot that sets different scales on the top and bottom axes as well as on left and right axes; it uses the axis command in the last line to specify against which axes the curves are plotted.

One problem with the graphs in this recipe is that, although there is a legend generated automatically to show which curve is a plot of which function, there is nothing to show us which curve is plotted against which axis. In *Chapter 2, Annotating with Labels and Legends*, you will see how to put informative labels and arrows on your plots to address this.

Making a scatterplot

If you are in possession of a collection of measurements that, as is usually the case, is subject to random errors, an attempt to simply plot a curve through the measurements may result in a chaotic graph that will be difficult to interpret. In these cases, one usually begins with a scatterplot, which is simply a plot of a dot or small symbol at each data point. An examination of such a plot often leads to the discovery of correlations or patterns.

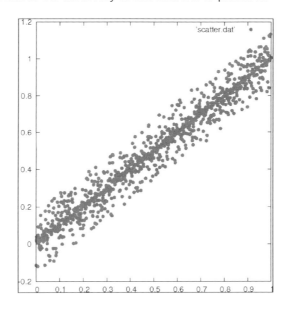

Getting ready

To make this recipe interesting, we need some slightly random-looking data. You may have some available, in which case you merely need to ensure that it is in a format that gnuplot can read. Simply arrange the data so that each line of the file contains one data point with space-separated *x* and *y* values:

```
x1  y1
x2  y2
. . .
```

Then name the file `scatter.dat`.

If you don't have such a file of your own handy, use the one called `scatter.dat` that we have provided. Make sure that the file is in the directory in which you have started gnuplot, so that the program can find it.

How to do it...

 Some of the recipes in this book will not work as intended if entered in the same interactive session unless you give the `reset` command first. This is because these scripts make settings that change gnuplot's default behavior.

Now simply tell gnuplot:

```
plot 'scatter.dat' with points pt 7
```

If you are using the file we provided, you will get a plot similar to the one shown in the previous figure.

There's more...

You can plot the points using different symbols. Try `plot 'scatter.dat' with dots` to get the smallest dot available to your terminal. For use with scatterplots of very large datasets, try the following command:

```
plot 'scatter.dat' with points pt n
```

With different integers for n. pt stands for **pointtype**, and the different pointtypes available are dependent on your terminal. Simply type `test` in gnuplot to see a demonstration of all the pointtypes available for the currently selected terminal. You can find more about point and line styles in *Chapter 3, Applying Colors and Styles*.

Plotting boxes

Gnuplot's box style is similar to a bar chart, with each value plotted as a box extending up from the axis. You can have the boxes filled with patterns, solid colors, or leave them empty.

This style is commonly used either as a type of histogram (covered later in this chapter) or as a way to compare a set of disparate items. The following figure plots boxes using the fill pattern:

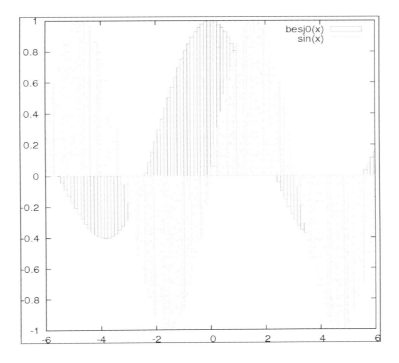

How to do it...

It just takes the following script to get the previous figure:

```
set style fill pattern
plot [-6:6]  besj0(x) with boxes, sin(x) with boxes
```

How it works...

The first command tells gnuplot to fill the boxes with a fill pattern, cycling through the patterns available on the selected output device for each plot on the graph. The second command plots the two specified functions using the boxes style, which draws a box from the x-axis to the y value for each point.

There's more...

You can specify empty boxes with `set style fill empty` or a solid color with `set style fill solid`, and of course you can select the fill style explicitly with `set style fill pattern n`, where n is any integer associated with a fill style in the selected terminal.

Plotting circles

This recipe will introduce gnuplot's ability to place objects at locations specified in a datafile or by mathematical functions, and to define their properties dynamically to convey information about the data. The following figure shows how gnuplot plots circles:

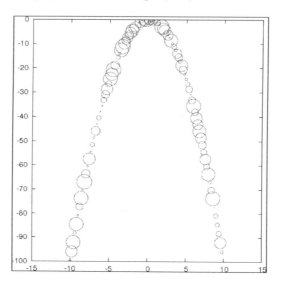

Getting ready

We have provided a datafile called `parabolaCircles.text`, which is similar to the `parabola.text` file that we created previously with gnuplot's help, but with a third column that consists of some random numbers. Make sure this file is in your current directory so that gnuplot can find it. Alternatively, use any datafile you like with three columns.

How to do it...

Enter the following script to make a circle plot:

```
set key off
plot "parabolaCircles.text" with circles
```

How it works...

For each point in the datafile, we get a circle with a radius determined by the number in the third column. Here the radii are random, but in practice you can encode some value of interest in the radii, in effect providing a way to plot two values for each point on the x-axis.

For example, the y coordinate can represent a measurement and the radii can indicate the uncertainty in the measurement; or we can get meteorological data and can plot temperature versus time, with the circle radius representing humidity.

The first line in the script turns off the legend that otherwise gnuplot adds by default.

Drawing filled curves

When you want to highlight the difference between two curves or datasets, or show when your data values exceed some reference value, the filled curve style, with some encouragement, can be made to serve. The following figure shows an example of filled curves:

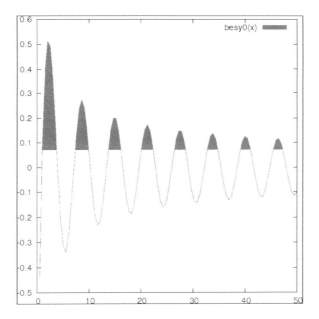

Getting ready

For the main recipe, you should be ready to go. If you want to try the commands for creating the second plot in this section, as shown in the next figure, you need another datafile `intersection`, which we have provided. This consists of the numerical output of a program that simply calculated the coordinates of a straight line and a parabola. You can substitute your own data, as long as it is the format described in the following _There's more..._ section.

How to do it...

The following command creates the previous figure:

```
plot [0:50] besy0(x) with filledcurves above y1=0.07
```

How it works...

This simple use of the **filledcurves** style colors in the area showing when the plotted Bessel function exceeds 0.07. We let gnuplot use the default color and shading style.

There's more...

You can change the color (to blue, for example) by appending lt rgb blue to the plotting command. If you want to change the fill style to use a pattern rather than a solid color, precede the plotting command with the following command:

```
set style fill pattern n
```

In this command n is an integer that specifies the fill style from those available in your terminal. To see a list of these, just issue the command test.

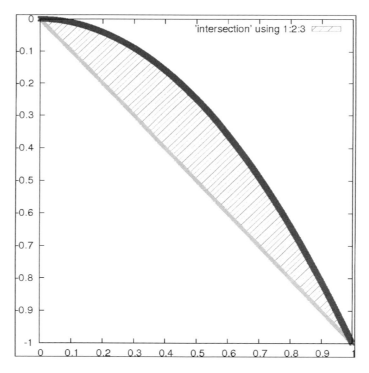

Suppose you are plotting data from a file, and the data is arranged in a table in the following format:

```
x1 y1 z1
x2 y2 z2
x3 y3 z3
. . .
```

You can fill in the difference between the two curves *y* versus *x* and *z* versus *x* with the following command:

```
plot <'file'> using 1:2:3 with filledcurves
```

Following is the complete script for creating the plot shown in the previous figure:

```
set style fill pattern 5
plot 'intersection' using 1:2:3 with filledcurves,\
   '' using 1:2 lw 3 notitle, '' using 1:3 lw 3 notitle
```

This plot shows the difference between a parabola and a straight line.

The fill pattern is similar to what you will get with the X11, Postscript, and some other terminals, but, as with all patterns and styles selected by an index number, this is dependent on the terminal. On the Macintosh using the Aquaterm terminal, for example, all the fill patterns are solid colors, and selecting an index merely changes the color.

The plot command used here exploits some features that we have not covered before. The `using` keyword selects the column from the datafile; `using 1:2:3` means to plot all columns, and the `filledcurves` style knows how to fill in the difference between the curves in this case. After this, we plot the parabola and line separately, using a blank filename to select the previous name. The purpose of the last two plot components of the command is to plot the thick lines that delimit the filled area; the `lw 3` chooses the line thickness, and the `notitle` tells gnuplot not to add an entry into the legend for these plot components, which would be redundant.

But what if you want to make something similar to the previous figure without making an intermediate datafile? You can make a plot that fills the area between two functions by using gnuplot's **special filenames**. This is a facility that allows you to do things that normally can only be done with datafiles right on the command line or in a script, without having to make a datafile.

Following is another way to get the previous figure:

```
set style fill pattern 5
plot [0:1] '+' using 1:(-$1):(-$1**2) with filledcurves,\
   -x lw 3 notitle, -x**2 lw 3 notitle
```

The + refers to a fictitious datafile where the first column consists of the automatically calculated sample points.

We've already encountered another of gnuplot's special files, the file called `' '` (an empty string), which refers to the previously named datafile, and we used it to avoid having to type its name multiple times.

Handling financial data

Although gnuplot was originally envisioned as a scientist's companion, it has proven to be a worthy and reliable friend to financial analysts. Financial plotting comes with its own set of complex problems, some of which we'll have to defer to later chapters; in the following figure, we illustrate the basic financial plotting style:

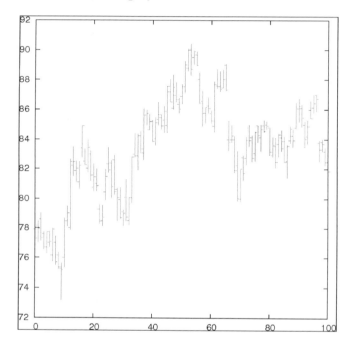

This type of plot will be familiar to you if you follow the stock market.

Getting ready

Sample financial data is essential for illustrating financial plotting. Fortunately, the gnuplot distribution comes with an appropriate sample datafile. In case you don't have it, we have provided a copy called `finance.dat`. Make sure it's in your current directory so that gnuplot can find it. You are welcome, of course, to use your own data, but it must be in the correct format. Each line of the file represents a separate data point, and consists of (at least) five numbers, separated by spaces: `date open low high close`.

An example of a line from such a datafile would look similar to the following:

```
3/11/2011   76.15   76.63   75.2   75.35
```

How to do it...

Enter the following commands while you are in the directory containing the datafile:

```
set bars 2
plot [0:100] 'finance.dat' using 0:2:3:4:5 notitle with financebars
```

How it works...

This makes the conventional financial graph showing the high, low, open, and close prices for a stock. If you are reading this recipe, you no doubt already know why you want this type of plot.

The default size of the tics for the opening and closing prices is quite small; the first command makes it longer. The second command sets the range, chooses the file, and specifies the columns to use for the finance plot.

Making a basic histogram plot

This recipe shows you how to make the simplest step-type histogram. Later, we will build histogram and statistical plots on this, but sometimes this is all you need. The following figure shows a simple step-type histogram:

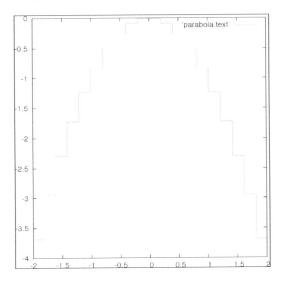

Getting ready

We're going to plot a part of our file `parabola.text`, so make sure that's still available. Of course, if you have your own sorted statistical data that will probably be more interesting.

How to do it...

Type the following command to make a histogram plot:

```
plot [-2:2] 'parabola.text' with histeps
```

How it works...

As we can see, rather than drawing a line through a series of *x-y* points, the histeps style draws a staircase composed of horizontal and vertical line segments. The vertical lines are drawn not at the actual *x*-coordinates given in the data, but at the average values of neighboring *x*-coordinates. This is the usual way to construct a histogram, where each box represents "how much" is contained in each interval between two *x*-values.

Stacking histograms

A more interesting type of histogram plot shows the distribution of some quantity with a second distribution stacked on top. This provides a quick way to visually compare two distributions. The values of the second distribution are measured not from the axis, but from the top of the box showing the first distribution. The following figure shows a stacking histogram:

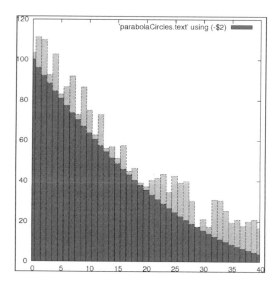

You might have noticed that the information printed in the legend on the upper-right corner is not very descriptive. This is the default; in the next chapter, you will learn how to change it to whatever you want.

Getting ready

We are going to reuse our datafile `parabolaCircles.text`.

How to do it...

The script that produced the stacked histogram is as follows:

```
set style fill solid 1.0 border lt -1
set style data histograms
set style histogram rowstacked
plot [0:40] 'parabolaCircles.text' using (-$2),\
    '' using (20*$3) notitle
```

How it works...

The first line requests histogram bars filled with a solid color, and with a black border. Without this, the bars are plotted unfilled, which makes the plot more difficult to interpret.

The next two lines specify that data from files should be plotted using histograms; the `rowstacked` style means that data from each row in the file will be plotted together in one vertical stack.

In the last line, we have chosen to illustrate how to do simple calculations on data columns; the expression is enclosed in parentheses, the column number is preceded with a dollar sign, and the familiar Fortran or C type syntax works just the way you would expect. So we have flipped our parabola back "right side up" with a negative sign, and increased the magnitude of our random numbers by multiplying by 20. (This file was used to plot circles with random diameters in the *Plotting circles* recipe in this chapter. The random numbers were scaled to give appropriately sized circles, but are too small to give a good illustration of the stacked histogram here. Rather than generating new data, some simple arithmetic allows us to reuse the file.)

Plotting multiple histograms

Rather than stacking the histograms, you can plot them side by side. The following figure shows the same data as in the previous plot, but has two separate sets of histograms plotted beside each other:

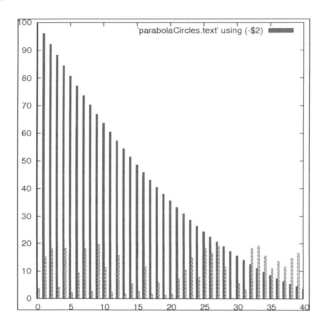

To make room, the histogram boxes are automatically drawn thinner. The different data sets are distinguished by different fill colors or patterns, depending on terminal, and/or different styles for the lines delineating the histogram boxes.

Getting ready

We are going to continue to wear out our datafile `parabolaCircles.text`.

How to do it...

Following are the commands used to produce a multiple histogram plot:

```
set style fill solid 1.0 border lt -1
set style data histograms
plot [0:40] 'parabolaCircles.text' using (-$2),\
   '' using (20*$3) notitle
```

How it works...

The shrewd reader will have noticed that this is the same recipe as the previous one, with the line `set style histogram rowstacked` removed. Here, we see the default multiple histogram style.

Dealing with errors

Along with data often comes error, uncertainty, or the general concept of a range of values associated with each plotted value. To express this in a plot, various conventions can be used; one of these is the "error bar", for which gnuplot has some special styles. The following figure shows an example of an error bar:

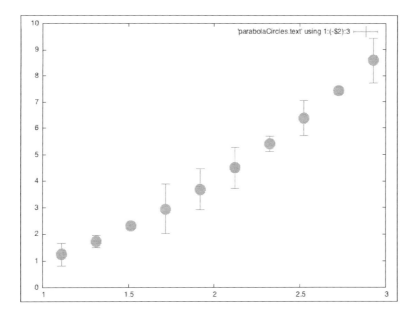

The previous figure has the same data that we used in our previous recipe, *Plotting circles*, plotted over a restricted range, and using the random number column to supply "errors", which are depicted here as vertical lines with small horizontal caps.

Getting ready

Keep the datafile `parabolaCircles.text` ready again.

How to do it...

Following is the script for producing a basic data set plot with `errorbars`:

```
set pointsize 3
set bars 3
plot [1:3] 'parabolaCircles.text' using 1:(-$2):3 with errorbars,\
   '' using 1:(-$2):3  pt 7 notitle
```

How it works...

We are using our trusty parabola plus the random number file again; here the random numbers will stand in for errors.

The default point size in gnuplot is quite small; the first line in the recipe increases this. This is especially important for presentations, where increasing the size of various plot elements will make your projected slides far easier to see. The second line increases the size of the small horizontal bars on the ends of the error bars; the default is rather small and hard to see. The third line selects the range, flips the parabola as before, and selects the error bars style. If we omit the portion after the comma, the error bars alone are plotted, with another small horizontal bar indicating the data values. This is OK, but the graph is easier to interpret if we plot a more distinct symbol at each data point; that's what the component after the comma does. We use the special file designator ` ` to mean the file already mentioned; `pt` is short for **point type**, and `pt 7` gives a solid circle on most terminals. Finally, `notitle` prevents a second, redundant entry in the legend.

There's more...

Error bars can be combined with some of the other plot styles. To create the following figure, which combines a box plot with error bars, change the last line in the recipe to the following commands:

```
set style fill pattern 2 border lt -1
plot [1:3] 'parabolaCircles.text' using 1:(-$2):3 with boxerrorbars
```

We've just changed `errorbars` to `boxerrorbars`, but first we set the fill pattern to a fine hatching pattern, (this will depend on your output device, try the command `test` to see them) and asked for a black border to be drawn around the boxes.

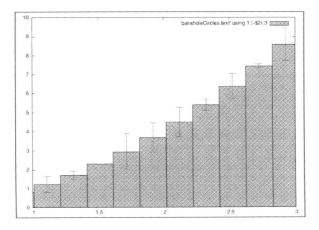

This is the same data plotted in the previous figure, in a different style.

Making a statistical whisker plot

Also known in the statistics world as a "box and whisker plot" or simply as a boxplot, the statistical whisker plot is a series of symbols, each one showing the mean value of a set of measurements, the extent of the central part of the measurements' or population's distribution, and the extent of the remainder of the distribution excluding the "outliers" (the outliers themselves are sometimes shown as dots, but we won't use that style here). This type of plot is also sometimes used for financial price data rather than the finance plot that was the subject of the *Handling financial data* recipe in this chapter. We will avoid the specialized language of statistics and further discussion of the uses of these plots, but the statisticians among our readers know why they're here. The following figure shows the depiction of a statistical whisker plot using gnuplot:

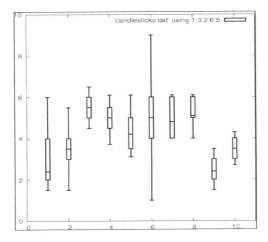

In the previous plot, typically, the boxes show the range of the central part of the data distribution; the short horizontal line within the boxes shows the value of the mean; and the vertical lines extending above and below the boxes show the range of the bulk of the distribution excluding the outliers.

Getting ready

We've borrowed the demo file `candlesticks.dat` that comes with the gnuplot distribution; make sure it's in your current directory. If you want to use your own data instead, each line of the file must be in the following format:

```
x   whisker_min   box_min   mean   box_high   whisker_high
```

How to do it...

Feed the following script to gnuplot to get the whisker plot:

```
set xrange [0:11]
set yrange [0:10]
set boxwidth 0.2
plot 'candlesticks.dat' using 1:3:2:6:5 with candlesticks lt -1 lw 2
whiskerbars, \
    '' using 1:4:4:4:4 with candlesticks lt -1 lw 2 notitle
```

How it works...

The first two lines set the x and y ranges of the axes; they are set to give a little room around the data. The next line sets the `boxwidth`—the width of the rectangle showing the extent of the central part of the distribution (the default is very skinny). Next comes the plot command, split here over two lines. The order of the fields expected by the candlestick style is x `box_min whisker_min whisker_high box_high`, which is not in the same order as our datafile, so we need to use the `using` command to put the columns in the right order for plotting. The first plot command also specifies the line type `lt` to be `-1` for solid black and a line width is set to 2; **whiskerbars** means put the little caps on the end of the whiskers. The second plot command—starting on the last line—plots from the same datafile, but employs a trick to use the 4th column—containing the mean value—repeatedly, effectively collapsing the box ends and whiskers down to the mean, all just to plot the little horizontal line in the middle of the boxes. This may seem like a convoluted method, but it ensures that the lines indicating the mean values are in the right places and have exactly the correct width to lie within the boxes.

There's more...

Some people prefer their whisker plot boxes to be filled in with a solid color or pattern. To get this, before issuing the plot command try the following command:

```
set style fill solid
```

or

```
set style fill pattern n
```

Making an impulse plot

Impulse or stick plots are another way to represent discrete points. If the line thickness is made large, the impulse plot can be made to look like a bar chart.

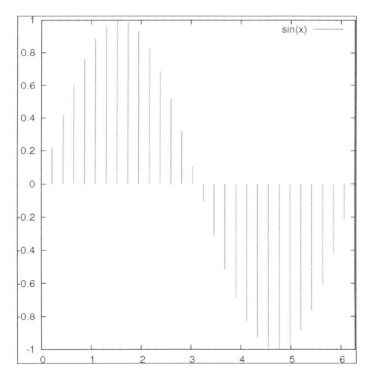

How to do it...

The following script illustrates the use of the `impulses` style:

```
set samples 30
plot [0:2*pi] sin(x) with impulses lw 2
```

How it works...

The first command set the number of points used to sample or plot the function. The plot command tells gnuplot to use the impulse style, which draws a line from the *x*-axis to each *y* value; the thickness of the line is given by `lw 2`.

There's more...

A "stem plot" is sometimes used in electrical engineering. It is similar to the impulse plot, but with a mark at the end of each stick; this allows the eye to more easily follow the trend of the data; conversely, the sticks make it easier to read the graph, especially when the data is sparse, compared with a simple point plot. Use the following recipe to create a stem plot of a decaying sine wave, illustrated in the following figure:

```
set samples 50
plot [0:4*pi] exp(-x/4.)*sin(x) with impulses lw 2 notitle,\
  exp(-x/4.)*sin(x) with points pt 7
```

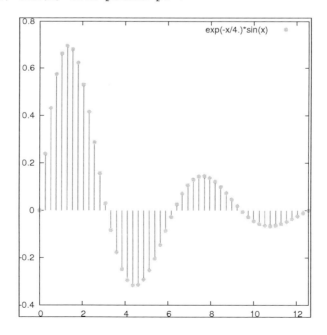

As you can see, we have plotted the same function twice. The first time through plot the impulses, as in the previous script, and the second time we plot the function again with `points` to draw the dots.

The previous plot shows a typical exponentially damped sine wave; it represents, for example, the motion of a pendulum with friction.

Graphing parametric curves

Gnuplot can graph functions whose *x* and *y* values depend on a third variable, called a **parameter**. In this way, more complicated curves can be drawn. The following plot resembles a lissajous figure, which can be seen on an oscilloscope when sine waves of different frequencies are controlling the *x* and *y* axes:

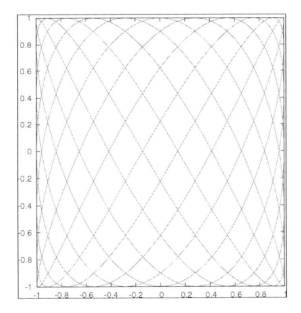

How to do it...

The following script creates the previous figure:

```
set samples 1000
set parametric
plot sin(7*t), cos(11*t) notitle
```

How it works...

We want more samples than the default 100 for a smoother plot, hence the first line. The second line (highlighted) changes the way gnuplot interprets plot commands; now the two functions (in the third line) are understood to provide *x* and *y* coordinates in the plane as the parameter t is varied. Once we say `set parametric`, then we can say `plot x(t), y(t)`, and the plot will trace out a curve given by x and y as t is varied between the limits given in **trange**.

There's more...

The range of values that t varies through to draw the plot defaults to `[-5:5]`. Try out different ranges to see what happens by setting the `trange`. For example, you can say `set trange [0:2]` and then `replot` to see the effect.

Plotting with polar coordinates

All the plots in this chapter up to now have implicitly used rectangular coordinates, usually denoted as *x* and *y*. For certain types of information, however, polar geometry is the natural coordinate system. In polar coordinates we have a radius, r, measured from the origin, usually at the center of the graph, and an angle, θ, usually measured counter-clockwise from the horizontal. On the gnuplot command line, the angular coordinate is called t by default. The following is an example of a spiral illustration:

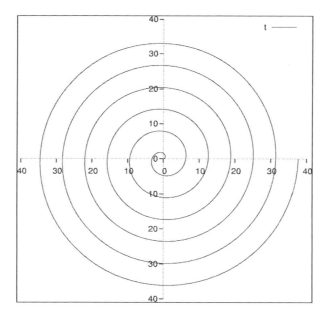

Using polar coordinates we can plot spirals and closed curves that are impossible to define explicitly using rectangular coordinates.

How to do it...

Following is an example of how to use polar coordinates to get the spiral shown in the previous illustration:

```
set xtics axis nomirror
set ytics axis nomirror
set zeroaxis
unset border
set samples 500
set polar
plot [0:12*pi] t
```

How it works...

The first three lines create a pair of axes that intersect at the origin in the center of the graph. This works for polar plots too, where we are measuring the radius from the center. The `unset border` line removes the frame that has served up to now as axes for our rectangular coordinate plots. Next, we increase the number of samples for a smooth plot. The crucial, highlighted line `set polar` changes to polar (r-θ) coordinates from the default rectangular (*x-y*). In the plot command, `t` is now a dummy variable that passes through the given angular range (default [0:2*pi], changed to [0:12*pi] here), and the provided function (`r`) is a function of `t`, in this case the identity, that yields a circular spiral.

2
Annotating with Labels and Legends

This chapter contains the following recipes:

- ► Labeling the axes
- ► Setting the label size
- ► Adding a legend
- ► Putting a box around the legend
- ► Adding a label with an arrow
- ► Using Unicode characters [new]
- ► Putting equations in your labels

Introduction

The graphs we created in the previous chapter served the purpose of illustrating the various 2D plot styles, but they were all missing a few things. For a graph to be useful in the real world, it must be endowed with a title and various labels that explain what it is about and how to interpret its assorted plot elements.

In this chapter, we revisit the 2D graph, creating one with a few curves, two different y-axes, and shaded areas, and in each recipe, we add an additional informative decoration to the plot. The graph remains the same, but in each recipe it will acquire more detailed annotation. This chapter is all about how to make these annotations, not about the plotting itself.

Labeling the axes

In this recipe, we add labels to our axes to explain what is being plotted and the significance of the tics and numerical scales. We also add an overall title that will appear at the top of the graph.

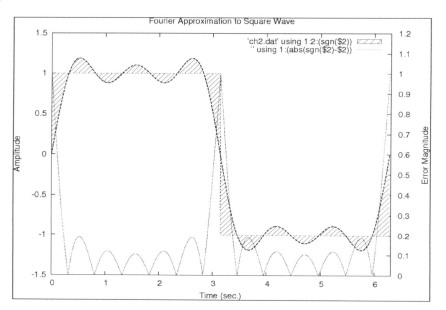

Make sure the supplied datafile ch2.dat is in your current directory. It is the result of adding the first three terms in the Fourier series approximation to the square wave. It is not important to understand what that means to follow the gnuplot recipes; we are using this file because it leads to a good graph for the purpose of illustrating annotations and labeling.

How to do it...

Following is the script that produces the previous annotated graph:

```
set yrange [-1.5:1.5]
set xrange [0:6.3]
set ytics nomirror
set y2tics 0,.1
set y2range [0:1.2]
set style fill pattern 5
set xlabel "Time (sec.)"
```

```
set ylabel "Amplitude"
set y2label "Error Magnitude"
set title "Fourier Approximation to Square Wave"
plot 'ch2.dat' using 1:2:(sgn($2)) with filledcurves,\
   '' using 1:2 with lines lw 2 notitle,\
   '' using 1:(sgn($2)) with lines notitle,\
   '' using 1:(abs(sgn($2)-$2)) with lines axis x1y2
```

How it works...

The highlighted lines in the code are the labeling commands being introduced in this recipe. The other commands are variations of code used in the recipes in the previous chapter. The `xlabel` and `ylabel` commands place the specified strings near the axes and should explain what the values on the axes mean, including units. The `y2label` command labels the right-hand "second" y-axis, if there is one. The `set title` command creates a title at the top of the graph.

There's more...

If you have a very long title (or label), gnuplot will not break it up into lines. It will just spill over into the margins of your graph and get truncated. You need to insert the line breaks manually by using the code `\n`, and make sure to surround your title string by double quotation marks. If you use single quotation marks, the `\n`s will be printed literally rather than being interpreted as the escape codes for a line break. For example, you can say `set title "Line One of a Very Long Title\nLine Two of the Title"`.

gnuplot centers the lines over the graph. If you find yourself constructing very long titles, however, you might consider moving some of that information into a caption or into the main text of your slide or document.

Setting the label size

The default font size for labels and titles in gnuplot looks a little small with most terminals. For example, the labels can be hard to read from the back rows of an auditorium during a presentation. We now show how to adjust the font size, and how to select the font for labels and titles.

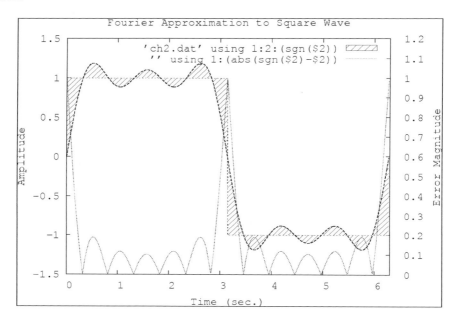

How to do it...

Most terminals accept a font and size specification in the `set terminal` command. To find out about the terminal you are using, just type `help set term terminal`, substituting the name of the terminal. For example, if you are using the PostScript terminal, typing `help set term postscript` provides a wealth of information on all the options accepted by the PostScript terminal, including the syntax for the font and size specifications. The following commands show how to produce the plot with all labels set in `Courier` at 18 pt:

```
set term postscript landscape "Courier, 18"
set output 'squarewave.ps'
set yrange [-1.5:1.5]
set xrange [0:6.3]
set ytics nomirror
set y2tics 0,.1
set y2range [0:1.2]
```

```
set style fill pattern 5
set xlabel "Time (sec.)
set ylabel "Amplitude"
set y2label "Error Magnitude"
set title "Fourier Approximation to Square Wave"
plot 'ch2.dat' using 1:2:(sgn($2)) with filledcurves,\
   '' using 1:2 with lines lw 2 notitle,\
   '' using 1:(sgn($2)) with lines notitle,\
   '' using 1:(abs(sgn($2)-$2)) with lines axis x1y2
```

How it works...

We've highlighted the new commands, which select the PostScript terminal and define a filename for the output. The first line chooses landscape orientation, which is usually desirable for single graphs standing on their own, and selects the Courier font at the somewhat larger-than-default 18 pt size. Note that this selects the font and size for the title, all labels, legend, and numbers labeling the tick marks. The second line says to put the output in the file `squarewave.ps`. You can choose any filename you like, as long as you place it within quotation marks. If you neglect to define an output, gnuplot will merrily spit out the PostScript code onto the terminal, which is probably not what you want.

There's more...

A few typographical changes to the graph make it easier on the eyes:

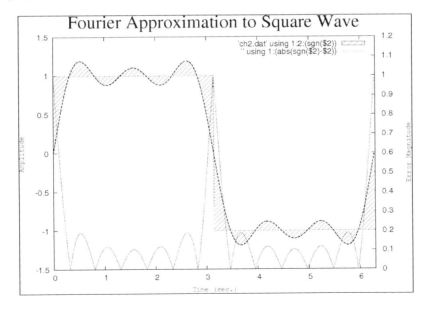

Having everything in the same style and size is neither very attractive nor optimally readable. Fortunately, we can select different fonts and sizes for every label and annotation on the graph:

```
set term postscript landscape
set yrange [-1.5:1.5]
set xrange [0:6.3]
set ytics nomirror
set y2tics 0,.1
set y2range [0:1.2]
set style fill pattern 5
set key font "Helvetica, 14"
set xlabel "Time (sec.)" font "Courier, 12"
set ylabel "Amplitude" font "Courier, 12"
set y2label "Error Magnitude" font "Courier, 12"
set title "Fourier Approximation to Square Wave" font "Times-Roman,
   32"
plot 'ch2.dat' using 1:2:(sgn($2)) with filledcurves,\
   ''   using 1:2 with lines lw 2 notitle,\
   '' using 1:(sgn($2)) with lines notitle,\
   '' using 1:(abs(sgn($2)-$2)) with lines axis x1y2
```

In the previous script, the font commands are highlighted. The fonts you request must be available on your computer; usually it is safe to use the familiar PostScript fonts, from which collection we have selected three typefaces in the example. The new `set key` command sets the style of the legend, which is the subject of the next recipe.

Adding a legend

The legend refers to the block of information printed on the graph (or occasionally outside it) that explains which curve or symbol is associated with which quantity. It is called a **key** in gnuplot. A legend or some device that conveys the equivalent information is essential when the graph displays more than one curve.

You've probably noticed that all of our example graphs already contain a key; this is done by gnuplot by default. This recipe will show you how to take complete control of your graph's legend.

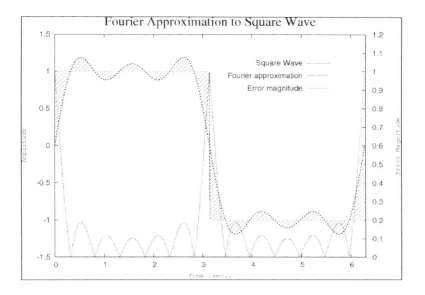

How to do it...

Following is a gnuplot script showing the extra commands that produce the legend in the previous plot:

```
set term postscript landscape
set yrange [-1.5:1.5]
set xrange [0:6.3]
set ytics nomirror
set y2tics 0,.1
set y2range [0:1.2]
set style fill pattern 5
set key at graph .9, .9 spacing 3 font "Helvetica, 14"
set xlabel "Time (sec.) font "Courier, 12"
set ylabel "Amplitude" font "Courier, 12"
set y2label "Error Magnitude" font "Courier, 12"
set title "Fourier Approximation to Square Wave" font "Times-Roman,
    4"
plot 'ch2.dat' using 1:2:(sgn($2)) with filledcurves notitle,\
   '' using 1:(sgn($2)) with lines title "Square Wave",\
   '' using 1:2 with lines lw 2 title "Fourier approximation",\
   '' using 1:(abs(sgn($2)-$2)) with lines axis x1y2 title "Error
   magnitude"
```

How it works...

The highlighted command defines some attributes for the key that result in an attractive and legible legend for our graph. The phrase at graph .9, .9 positions the key at location x = y = 0.9 in **graph coordinates**, which is a coordinate system where (0,0) is at the bottom left of the actual graph (not the screen on which the graph is drawn). Ask gnuplot for help coordinate to get a rundown of the *five* coordinate systems available to you. The phrase spacing 3 increases the vertical space between the lines over the default of 1.25. The spacing and positioning commands are set to be different from the defaults because we have some extra room in part of the graph that we can take advantage of to make our legend more attractive.

The other changes in the recipe are in the plot commands. Now, each component of the plot command ends with either a **title** phrase or with the keyword **notitle**. These phrases are used in the legend, and allow you to define more descriptive tags for your curves rather than the usually useless ones used by default, which, as you've seen, are derived by gnuplot automatically from the using clauses and the names of the datafiles.

There's more...

When there is no room inside the graph for the legend, or when you prefer this style for other reasons, you can put the key outside the graph:

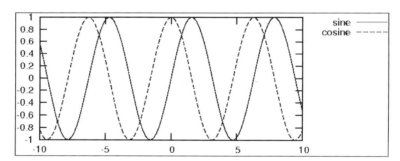

The previous little graph was made with the following commands:

```
set term postscript landscape size 5,2 "Helvetica, 9"
set key outside
plot sin(x) title "sine", cos(x) title "cosine"
```

When you are setting the size of the PostScript terminal, you often have to reset the overall font size, as it does not scale with the graph size.

Putting a box around the legend

This recipe is a simple modification of the previous one, but gets its own section because the legend in the box is such a popular style (for better or worse).

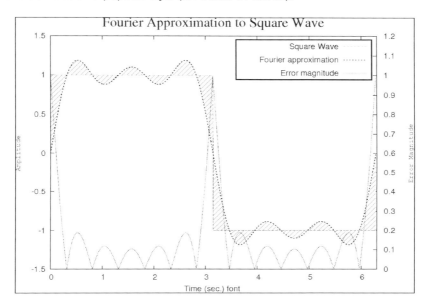

How to do it...

Replace the highlighted set key command in the previous recipe with the following two commands:

```
set key spacing 3 font "Helvetica, 14"
set key box lt -1 lw 2
```

How it works...

The new command is in the second line. set key box tells gnuplot to draw a box around the legend; this is followed by two specifications for the type of line from which the box will be drawn. In the previous command, we have used abbreviations: lt stands for **linetype**, and a linetype of -1 yields a solid black line in the PostScript terminal. lw stands for **linewidth**; lw 2 is one step up from the default lw 1, and makes the box more prominent.

Adding a label with an arrow

Complex graphs can often benefit from information in addition to what can be provided in a title, in the axis labels, and a legend. Sometimes we need to explain the meaning of a particular feature on the graph. This can be done with labels and arrows.

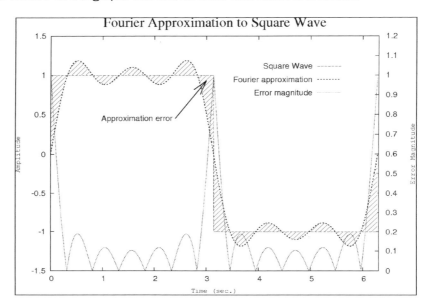

How to do it...

Following is the complete script that you can feed to gnuplot to create the graph:

```
set term postscript landscape
set out 'fourier.ps'
set yrange [-1.5:1.5]
set xrange [0:6.3]
set ytics nomirror
set y2tics 0,.1
set y2range [0:1.2]
set style fill pattern 5
set key at graph .9, .9 spacing 3 font "Helvetica, 14"
set xlabel "Time (sec.)" font "Courier, 12"
set ylabel "Amplitude" font "Courier, 12"
set y2label "Error Magnitude" font "Courier, 12"
set title "Fourier Approximation to Square Wave" font "Times-Roman,
  24"
set label "Approximation error" right at 2.4, 0.45 offset -.5, 0
```

```
set arrow 1 from first 2.4, 0.45 to 3, 0.93 lt 1 lw 2 front size .3,
   15
plot 'ch2.dat' using 1:2:(sgn($2)) with filledcurves notitle,\
   '' using 1:(sgn($2)) with lines title "Square Wave",\
   '' using 1:2 with lines lw 2 title "Fourier approximation",\
   '' using 1:(abs(sgn($2)-$2)) with lines axis x1y2 title "Error
   magnitude"
```

How it works...

We have highlighted two new commands that together supply some additional annotation to our graph. The first highlighted command places a label with text given in quotation marks immediately following the words `set label`. The phrase `right at 2.4, 0.45` places the label *right justified* at x = 2.4 and y = 0.45 using the **first coordinate system**. The use of this coordinate system is the default and is convenient, because the point can be read directly from the graph `axis`. `first` means that we are using the left-hand y-axis; the second coordinate system is also available, which uses the right and bottom axes. The **offset** parameters shift the label by the amount given in the *x* and *y* directions using the **character coordinate system**. The values used in the script shift the label to the left by half a character width, creating a small space between the end of the label and the beginning of the shaft of the arrow. Finally, we set the font and type size for the label. (In place of the keyword `right`, we also have `center` and `left` available, which create their respective justifications.)

The second new command draws an arrow, which we have given a **tag** of 1, from a starting point at x = `2.4`, y = `0.45` in the first coordinate system (the same point at which our text label was right justified to) to an ending point in the hatched region at x = 3, y = `0.93`. The rest of the arrow specifications set its line type (`lt`) and line width (`lw`), tell gnuplot to plot the arrow on top of the graph data (`front`), and give the **size** of the arrowhead: the first number, `.3`, is the length of the sides of the head in graph units; the second, `15`, is the number of degrees of angle from the shaft of the arrow to the head.

It is usually impossible to get the positioning of the labels and arrows correct on the first try. One usually resorts to repeatedly making plots while adjusting the positioning coordinates until everything looks right. The `tag` in the `set arrow` command allows you to change the details of the existing arrow, simply by issuing another `set arrow 1`. Without this tag, gnuplot would simply create a new arrow. If you want to adjust the positioning of your labels, say `unset label`, and repeat the labeling commands with new parameters, or use tags for your labels as we did for the arrow and simply redefine them. In this way, you can iterate, issuing a `replot` command after each arrow and label definition, until the plot looks the way you like it. Then, if you want to save your plot, use the `set output` command to open a file for output, and reissue your `plot` command.

Using Unicode characters [new]

A new feature in gnuplot 4.4 allows you to use the **Unicode** character set in your graph's title and labels. This is a vast improvement over more cumbersome methods of entering special characters, but it does not work on all terminals. For example, PostScript does not support Unicode directly, but some implementations of the pdf and png terminals, and others, will work. The following example was created using the `pngcairo` version of the png terminal. Which versions you have available will depend on the details of your operating system and gnuplot installation. A more general method for creating complex labels is given in the next recipe.

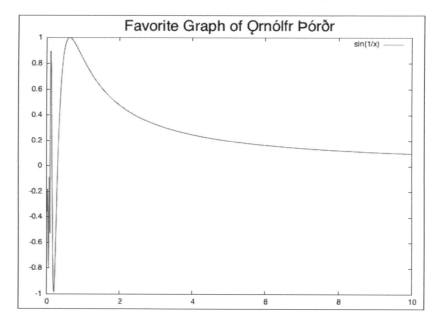

Getting ready

You will need some method of inputting Unicode characters. There are myriad ways of doing this, depending on your operating system, terminal program, text editor, and so on, and the details are beyond the scope of this book. In order to create the title for this example, incorporating the name of a famous Viking scientist, we merely copied the name from a web page and pasted it into the command line; this may or may not work, depending on the details of your setup.

How to do it...

One extra command lets us use Unicode. Following is the script that gets us the previous plot:

```
set term png
set samples 500
set encoding utf8
set title "Favorite Graph of Ǫrnólfr Þórðr" font "Helvetica, 24"
plot [0:10] sin(1/x)
```

How it works...

First, you need to set the terminal to something that supports Unicode. You may need to simply try some of the terminals available in your gnuplot compilation; if the title in the final graph looks similar to the input, it worked. If Unicode is not properly supported, gnuplot may not complain, but there will be gibberish on your graph. It may very well be that there is no terminal available in your gnuplot installation that supports Unicode input. But, in a later chapter, we will learn far more flexible and sophisticated methods for including text of arbitrary complexity in the graph, and in the next recipe we shall see how to use special codes to input some symbols, Greek letters, and so on—so there are several alternatives. Terminals that are known by me to support Unicode are the Cairo png, svg, and Aquaterm terminals; PostScript does not work. The highlighted line is the essential command that tells gnuplot to handle Unicode input. Then simply enter the Unicode strings directly.

Putting equations in your labels

Certain terminals support **enhanced text**, which means that they accept a markup language specific to gnuplot that can be used to include characters from various fonts, set subscripts, superscripts, overprint characters, and generally manipulate text with sufficient flexibility to create simple equations to serve as annotations for your graphs. This recipe shows how to make such an equation, but you will see that the markup is cumbersome, and attaining the desired result requires some amount of trial and error. Frankly, a better way to create all but the simplest mathematical text is to use the LaTeX techniques covered in a later chapter, which also leads to a much more attractive output.

However, the enhanced text mode can be useful for quickly placing some mathematical text on your plot, in situations where you are not too picky about the typographical quality of the result.

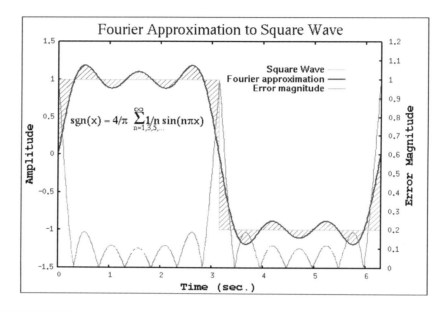

How to do it...

The following script is similar to the script in the *Adding a label with an arrow* recipe in this chapter; only the set term command and the label commands have been changed:

```
set term x11 enhanced
set yrange [-1.5:1.5]
set xrange [0:6.3]
set ytics nomirror
set y2tics 0,.1
set y2range [0:1.2]
set style fill pattern 5
set key at graph .9, .9 spacing 3 font "Helvetica, 14"
set xlabel "Time (sec.)" font "Courier, 18"
set ylabel "Amplitude" font "Courier, 18"
set y2label "Error Magnitude" font "Courier, 18"
set title "Fourier Approximation to Square Wave" font "Times-Roman,
   24"
set label \
   "sgn(x) = 4/{/Symbol p}&{x}~{~@{/Symbol=24 S}{-
   .5/*.7n=1,3,5,...}}{.9/Symbol=18 \245}&
   {xx}1/n sin(n{/Symbol p}x)" \font "Times-Roman, 18"
```

```
        at graph .04, .65
    plot 'ch2.dat' using 1:2:(sgn($2)) with filledcurves notitle,\
        '' using 1:(sgn($2)) with lines title "Square Wave",\
        '' using 1:2 with lines lw 2 title "Fourier approximation",\
        '' using 1:(abs(sgn($2)-$2)) with lines axis x1y2 title "Error
        magnitude"
```

How it works...

For a full rundown on the markup syntax for enhanced text, type `help enhanced` at the interactive gnuplot prompt. We'll explain the subset of the syntax we used to create this equation, which gives the Fourier series for a square wave. The `/Symbol` tags select the Symbol font; `p` in this font is the Greek letter pi, and `S` is the capital Greek sigma, meaning sum. The `&{xx}` notation means to insert a space equal to two "x"s. The notation `@X` means that the character "X" is to be counted as taking up no space. The notation `~a{.7b}` means to overprint `a` with `b` raised `.7` times the line height; we use it with a construction in curly brackets rather than a single character. The infinity symbol is selected with `/Symbol=18 \245`, which means select character number `245` from the Symbol font at size `18` pt.

 If you find that the markup codes have been copied as written to the graph, rather than interpreted similarly to the figure, then you might have forgotten to say "enhanced" as part of your `set term` command.

We created this graph with the X11 terminal; experiments with other terminals reveal that the spacing might change, and more trial and error will be needed. This is another reason why the LaTeX methods explained later in the book are preferable, as they create exactly the same output under all conditions.

3
Applying Colors and Styles

This chapter contains the following recipes:

- ▶ Coloring your curves
- ▶ Styling your curves
- ▶ Applying transparency [new]
- ▶ Plotting points with curves
- ▶ Changing the point style
- ▶ Changing the plot size
- ▶ Positioning graphs on the page [new]
- ▶ Plotting with objects [new]

Introduction

This chapter is mostly concerned with ways to tell the different curves apart when multiple functions and/or datasets are plotted on a single graph. The three chief methods of accomplishing this are to plot the curves with different colors, different styles (thin, thick, dashed, dotted, and so on), or by using different types of symbols (or what gnuplot calls `points`). We saw examples of different `line styles` in the preceding chapters, and gnuplot will automatically render a series of curves in a succession of styles or colors in order to distinguish them. But now we will learn the details of how to take charge of our line styles, colors, and point styles. The printed version of this book will not let you see the full effect of manipulating color, but the electronically available versions of the graphs contain all the color and transparency information resulting from the recipes.

In addition to colors and styles, this chapter discusses setting the size of your plot, and introduces three new features of gnuplot 4.4: transparency, new semantics for graph positioning, and plotting with objects.

Coloring your curves

The following figure is a simple graph of different powers of x, color-coded. The colors, which can be seen in the electronic version of the graph, appear here as different shades of gray:

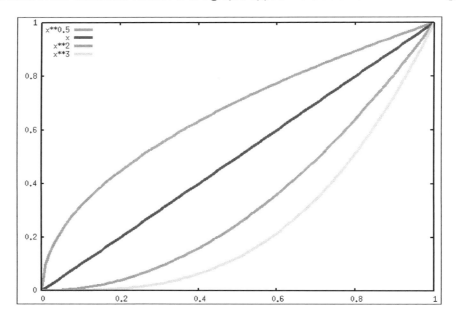

How to do it...

To produce the previous figure, enter the following sequence of commands at the gnuplot interactive prompt. Alternatively, save them in a file and use the command `gnuplot --persist <file>`, substituting your filename for `<file>`. The `--persist` flag tells gnuplot to keep the plot window open after executing the script. (This script, as well as all the others, are provided with this book as a file named after the recipe.)

```
set term x11 solid lw 4
set border lw .25
set key top left
plot [0:1] x**0.5 lc rgb 'orange', x lc rgb 'steelblue',\
           x**2 lc rgb 'bisque', x**3  lc rgb 'seagreen'
```

How it works...

In the first line we have chosen the X11 terminal and specified some terminal options. The interactive X11 terminal is usually available on Linux and other Unix-like systems, including the Macintosh if X11 is installed, which it likely will be for scientific or engineering work. However, this example will work on most gnuplot terminals.

 Setting terminal **defaults** at the beginning will save us the trouble of repeatedly specifying the same things in every subsequent plot command.

The words `solid lw 4` specify that solid lines are to be used, rather than a sequence of line types with different dash and dot patterns, and that the **linewidth**, abbreviated here as `lw`, is set to `4`. What this linewidth actually translates to on the screen or paper depends on the terminal. The gnuplot command `test`, which must be entered before any terminal options are set, will help us here. The reason you must execute the `test` command without any other styling options is that certain aspects of the `test` command output are shown *relative* to the options in force. So if you use the options we mentioned, the display of linewidths will all be approximately four times thicker than normal.

Setting the default linewidth affects all the lines in the plot, so we need to undo this where we don't want it. We want extra thick curves, but normal axis borders and tic marks. So, in the second line we set the border linewidth to `1/4`, to undo the effect of setting the overall linewidth to `4`.

The plot commands contain the new phrases `lc rgb 'orange'`, and so on. As you might have guessed, `lc` is an abbreviation for **linecolor**. These phrases set the colors for the curves, using gnuplot's color names. To see a list of these names, just type `show colors` at the gnuplot command prompt. The `rgb` keyword means that what follows is a red-green-blue color specification.

There's more...

If you tried out the `show colors` command, you might have noticed some additional columns after the column of workaday and fanciful color names. These are the numerical rgb values corresponding to the color names, first in a special **hexadecimal** format, then in decimal, where each color (red, green, or blue) can range in value from 0 to 255. So, for example, `seagreen` has the values red = 193, green = 255, blue = 193. The hexadecimal coding uses pairs of hexadecimal digits to represent the red, green, and blue values, in that order. Using the `seagreen` example for illustration, c1 = 193 in hex, ff = 255, and c1 = 193. This is exactly the same convention used in web design for the specification of colors in stylesheets and elsewhere, including the leading "#" as a signal that a hexadecimal color value follows. For serious work, it is probably a better idea to use numerical rgb color specifications rather than the color names.

This is because it provides you with more control, allows you to choose from the entire gamut of over 16 million colors, and lends itself to automation, where color values can be chosen algorithmically to maintain a relationship to the data plotted. Remember that the numerical code must be quoted, just as the color names are. `plot sin(x) lc rgb '#cc00cc'` is the correct form for a purple sine wave.

Styling your curves

This recipe delves into more detail about the **linetypes** we've seen before and introduces the powerful concept of **linestyles**.

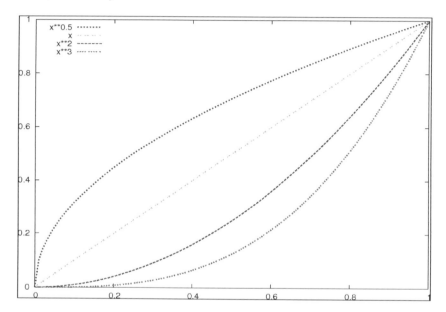

How to do it...

Following is the script that makes the previous figure:

```
set key top left
set style line 1 lt 3 lw 4 lc rgb '#990042'
set style line 2 lt 7 lw 3 lc rgb '#31f120'
set style line 3 lt 2 lw 3 lc rgb '#0044a5'
set style line 4 lt 9 lw 4 lc rgb '#888888'
plot [0:1] x**0.5 ls 1, x ls 2, x**2 ls 3, x**3 ls 4
```

How it works...

In this recipe, we have introduced **userstyles**. With the invocation `set style line n` you can define a set of properties that will be associated with the index n in subsequent `plot` commands. In order to call up these properties, simply append the phrase `ls n`, substituting the desired index for n, to the plot command. `ls` is an abbreviation for **linestyle**.

The advantages of linestyles are that they can be reused repeatedly, can save considerable typing or space in gnuplot scripts, and can help to organize your scripts while making them easier to read.

In the recipe, we have selected a linetype (`lt`), linewidth (`lw`), and linecolor for each user-defined linestyle. The linewidths and linecolors are terminal independent, but the particular dash and dot pattern, if any, corresponding to each linetype depends entirely on the terminal in use, and the options selected in the `set terminal` command. The illustration for this recipe used the PostScript terminal (translated eventually into a PNG file for printing in this book), which has a good selection of dash and dot styles. Some terminals, such as Aquaterm for the Macintosh, offer only solid lines; the X11 terminal— commonly used for interactive work with Linux—only offers line patterns if the X Window system is specially configured, and they are not rendered as well as they are by PostScript.

There's more...

We have seen many times how gnuplot automatically uses a sequence of line types (which may appear as different dash-dot patterns or merely as different colors, depending on the terminal in use and the default options passed to it) when plotting more than one thing, in order to distinguish the various functions or data sets plotted on the graph. Now that we know how to define our own styles for curves, we may want to use our user styles in an automatic sequence rather than the choices gnuplot makes by default, and without having to specify the `linestyle` manually for each curve. To do this, enter `set style increment userstyles` before the plotting commands, and gnuplot will cycle through your defined `linestyles` rather than the terminal's default `linetypes`. To return to the default behavior, enter `set style increment default`.

Applying transparency [new]

As of version 4.4, gnuplot supports **transparency**, which allows us to create attractive and sophisticated effects by setting the **opacity** of colors in various contexts. This technique is most useful when drawing with styles such as `filledcurves` using areas of solid color:

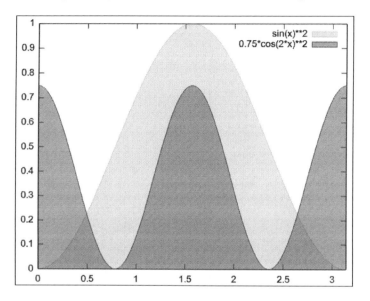

How to do it...

The following script will produce the previous figure:

```
set term svg
set out 'file.svg'
set style fill transparent solid 0.3
plot [0:pi] sin(x)**2 with filledcurves above y1=0 lc rgb  '#00ffff',\
    0.75*cos(2*x)**2 with filledcurves above y1=0 lc rgb '#aa00aa'
```

How it works...

We have included an explicit `set term` command in this recipe because transparency effects are only supported so far by a limited number of terminals. The `SVG` terminal is a recent addition to the gnuplot repertoire and is the new standard for resolution independent graphics on the Web; it has full support for transparency and produces high quality renderings that scale to any size without pixelation. Also, an SVG graph is an XML file that can be edited in a pinch and included inline in xhtml webpages.

You must remember that the file is not completely written out (the final SVG closing tag is missing) until either gnuplot is quit or another `set out` command is issued, as gnuplot does not know whether additional plotting commands are coming.

The highlighted line sets the fill style to be **solid** (rather than a pattern) and selects transparency with an opacity of `0.3`, where an opacity of `0` is invisible and an opacity of `1` is opaque. The subsequent plotting commands should be familiar; we have used the `filledcurves` style from *Chapter 1, Plotting Curves, Boxes, Points, and more* and specified colors as explained in the earlier recipe *Color your curves*.

There's more...

Patterns can be transparent, too. Instead of saying `set style fill transparent solid 0.3` we can say `set style fill transparency pattern n`, where the desired fill pattern is substituted for `n`. This will allow plot elements to appear behind fill patterns, showing through the "spaces" in the patterns. If used with care this can be useful, but can easily lead to a confusing or busy graph compared with the clean effect of transparent solid colors. Also, this is only supported by certain terminals, and not the same set that supports transparent colors. For example, the PostScript terminal supports transparent patterns, but not colors; the svg terminal does not support transparent patterns.

Plotting points with curves

In addition to the two main styles we have encountered for the plotting of 2D data or functions—namely a curve or a series of markers—gnuplot offers a third style consisting of a curve overlaid with markers. This style is useful in plotting tabulated data, where different marker styles can be used to distinguish between different data sets and the smooth line connecting them serves to guide the eye. The **linespoints** style is also favored by some even when plotting mathematical functions, where different marker styles are used to indicate the function being plotted rather than different line types (dot and dash patterns).

The next recipe shows in detail how to select these various marker styles; here we introduce the use of the linespoints plotting style.

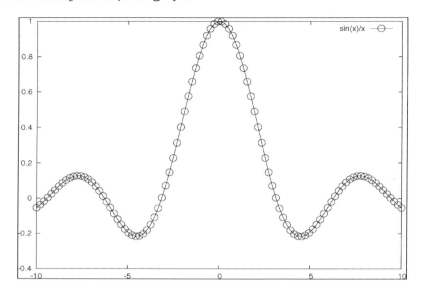

How to do it...

The following command creates the previous figure:

```
plot sin(x)/x with linespoints ps 2 pt 6
```

How it works...

We select the linespoints style with the phrase with linespoints. The expression ps 2 selects a **pointsize** approximately twice as large as the default, and the expression pt 6 selects the **pointtype** index 6. What this looks like depends entirely on the terminal in use; the open circle shown here is what you get with the PostScript terminal.

Changing the point style

In this section, we extend the use of user styles introduced in the earlier recipe *Styling your curves* to defining user styles for markers for use with the linespoints type of plots introduced in the previous recipe.

How to do it...

There are some more style choices that can be made part of the user-defined linestyles when you are plotting using the `linespoints` style, which draws a series of markers, or "points", along the line. This works best with solid lines, as shown in the figure following the commands:

```
set term postscript landscape color solid
set out 'file.ps'
set key top left
set style function linespoints
set style line 1 lw 4 lc rgb '#990042' ps 2 pt 6 pi 5
set style line 2 lw 3 lc rgb '#31f120' ps 2 pt 12 pi 3
set style line 3 lw 3 lc rgb '#0044a5' ps 2 pt 9 pi 5
set style line 4 lw 4 lc rgb '#888888' ps 2 pt 7 pi 4
plot [0:1] x**0.5 ls 1, x ls 2, x**2 ls 3, x**3 ls 4
```

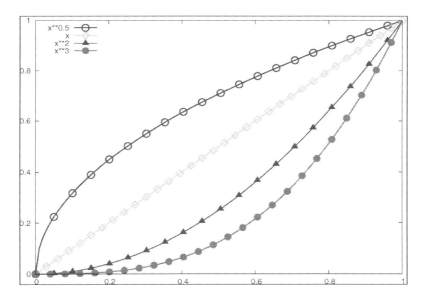

How it works...

The abbreviation `ps` stands for **pointsize**, which sets the size of the marker; `pt` refers to **pointtype**, which selects from the set of marker styles that you can see when you type `test`, and `pi` stands for **pointinterval**, which tells the program how often to place a marker along the line. The default pointinterval of `1` draws a marker at each calculated point, which can make for a crowded graph, or even a solid mass if the **samples** parameter is set to a large number.

Changing the plot size

The size of the graph is specified as a **size** option to the `set term` command. The exact interpretation of this option may vary between terminals, and has changed in recent versions of gnuplot. We'll give an example of its most recent usage in gnuplot 4.4. The following figure illustrates the use of the size option in gnuplot:

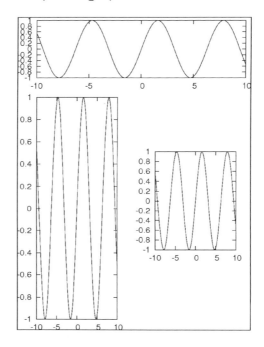

How to do it...

The figure consists of three separate files created by gnuplot using the following recipe:

```
unset key
set term postscript size 6,2
set out 'p1.ps'
plot sin(x)
set term postscript size 5,5
set out 'p2.ps'
plot sin(x)
set term postscript size 3,6
set out 'p3.ps'
plot sin(x)
```

How it works...

First we turn off the legend, which gets in the way of the plots in this example. The `set term` commands each have a single `size` option, which sets the horizontal and vertical extents of the graphs in inches. Each plot is saved to a separate file with a `set out` command; the files were assembled in a graphics program into the figure. In general, especially when working with resolution independent files such as PostScript, the absolute size of the graph has little meaning, and the main use of the `size` option is to define the **aspect ratio** of the graph. We have illustrated that in this recipe by creating the same plot using three different aspect ratios.

Positioning graphs on the page [new]

A new feature of gnuplot 4.4 is the more consistent handling of the concepts of graph and canvas sizes. This allows more predictable positioning of graphs on the output page, or canvas.

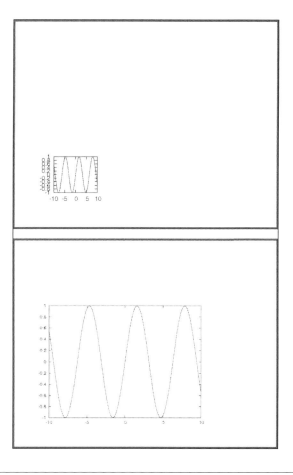

How to do it...

The two pages shown in the previous figure were made with the following script:

```
unset key
set size .75,.75
set out 'file1'
plot sin(x)
set size .25,.25
set out 'file2'
plot sin(x)
```

How it works...

Here, in the highlighted code lines, we have set the **sizes** of the plots. The size runs from 0 to 1, where 1 is the usual default that fills the entire canvas with the graph. The figure shows the results as they would appear if printed out, on an actual piece of paper, in most terminals. A thick border is drawn to indicate the paper boundaries; we see that the plot is anchored to the lower left-hand side. The graph sizes are distinct from the size option given to the set term command that we discussed in the previous recipe, which generally determines the size of the canvas. Note that the precise effects of the terminal size option and the set size command, and their interaction, may vary somewhat between terminals. In particular, the behavior of the PostScript terminal is in flux in recent patch levels of gnuplot 4.4.

Plotting with objects [new]

The latest version of gnuplot has some new commands for plotting with **objects**, which are geometrical shapes including rectangles, circles, ellipses, and polygons. In order to show off the flexibility of gnuplot's new object plotting commands, we have abused them in order to create something that is not part of gnuplot's normal repertoire: a pie chart. The following is a pie chart made using objects in gnuplot:

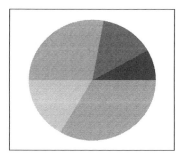

How to do it...

Following is the dark magic that can coerce gnuplot to render the previous figure:

```
unset key
unset tics
set object 1 circle at graph .5,.5 size graph .25 fillcolor rgb 'blue'
fillstyle solid \
   arc [0:30] front
set object 2 circle at graph .5,.5 size graph .25 fillcolor rgb 'red'
fillstyle solid \
   arc [30:80] front
set object 3 circle at graph .5,.5 size graph .25 fillcolor rgb
'orange' fillstyle solid \
   arc [80:180] front
set object 4 circle at graph .5,.5 size graph .25 fillcolor rgb
'green' fillstyle solid \
   arc [180:240] front
set object 5 circle at graph .5,.5 size graph .25 fillcolor rgb
'sandybrown' fillstyle solid \
   arc [240:360] front
plot [0:1][0:1] -1
```

How it works...

First we have instructed gnuplot to leave out the legend, the tics and tic labels. The next set of commands defines five `objects`, each with a unique index number that allows us to redefine or undefine it later. We want the objects to be circles, and set their sizes and positions using the graph coordinate system. Each circle is centered in the middle of the graph and has a radius equal to a quarter of the graph's extent. Each circle is given a different color using gnuplot's color names, and we have asked the circles to be filled in with solid colors. Finally, each circle is given an `arc` specification that runs in degrees clockwise from the positive x direction. This makes each circle into a wedge, and we've made the starting angle of each circle equal to the ending angle of the previous one, so that there are no gaps between them. The final keyword `front` forces the objects to be plotted on top of any other plot elements. In order to actually draw these objects, we need to issue a plot command; since we want nothing else on the graph we've constructed one that won't produce anything visible. The final line in the script does this by plotting a number outside of the range specified in the square brackets. Of course, a real pie chart would have labels explaining each wedge, which we can add using the techniques from the previous chapter.

4
Controlling your Tics

This chapter contains the following recipes:

- ▶ Adding minor tics
- ▶ Placing tics on the second y-axis
- ▶ Adjusting the tic size
- ▶ Removing all tics
- ▶ Defining the tic values
- ▶ Making the tics stick out
- ▶ Setting manual tics
- ▶ Plotting with dates and times
- ▶ Changing the language used for labels [new]
- ▶ Using European-style decimals [new]
- ▶ Formatting tic labels

Introduction

The recipes in this chapter deal with a notoriously tricky subject: how to get your tic marks and labels just right. Along the way, we learn about some of gnuplot's new internationalization features.

The tic labels we refer to here are the ones intimately associated with tic marks on the axes. What gnuplot calls "labels" are the annotations that we covered in the previous chapter.

Adding minor tics

Here is a simple plot with some extra elements that we haven't seen before. There are smaller tic marks between the major, labeled tic marks. These are referred to as minor tics. There is also a grid of dotted lines covering the graph, with the grid lines aligned with the major tic marks.

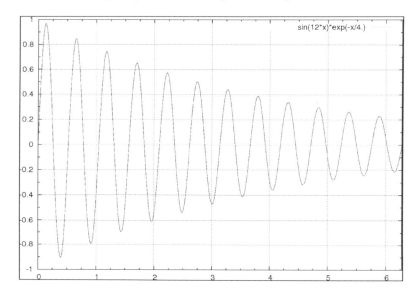

How to do it...

The following script will create the previous figure:

```
set grid
set mxtics 4
set mytics 2
plot [0:2*pi] sin(12*x)*exp(-x/4)
```

How it works...

The new commands are in the highlighted lines. set grid causes the light grid lines to appear when we finally issue the plot command. The second and third lines create **minor tics** on the axes. mxtics sets the minor tics on the x-axis and mytics creates minor tics on the y-axis. The number following the keyword (mxtics or mytics) sets the number of spaces between tics rather than the actual number of minor tics. Examining the figure should make it clear how this works. The purpose of minor tics is to make it easier for the reader to extract quantitative information from the graph by making it easier to interpolate between the numerically labeled values associated with the major tic marks.

Placing tics on the second y-axis

In this recipe, we revisit the technique introduced in *Chapter 1, Plotting Curves, Boxes, Points, and more* for plotting two curves on one graph, each with its own independent *y*-axis. The following figure provides an example for this recipe:

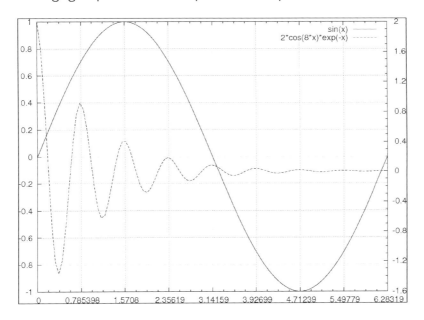

How to do it...

Run the following script through gnuplot to produce the previous figure:

```
set ytics nomirror
set y2tics 0.4
set my2tics 4
set xtics pi/4.
set mxtics 4
set grid
plot [0:2*pi] sin(x) axis x1y1, 2*cos(8*x)*exp(-x) axis x1y2
```

How it works...

As we saw in *Chapter 1, Plotting Curves, Boxes, Points, and more*, the command `set ytics nomirror` tells gnuplot to not duplicate the tics on the left (y1) axis with the tics on the right (y2) axis. This allows us to use two independent scales so we can plot two curves with different ranges on the same graph. However, we must explicitly tell gnuplot what tic interval to use on the y2 axis, or it will simply omit the tics there. This is the purpose of the second code line, which sets the tic spacing to `0.4`. The third, highlighted, line, sets the minor tics for the y2 axis. Note that we have set the major tic interval on the x-axis to be based on `pi`, this aligns the tics with the peaks in the circular function plotted, and is more meaningful here than using a rational interval.

Adjusting the tic size

The default length gnuplot uses for tics is a little small, and makes the minor tics all but disappear on small plots. Naturally, the tic size can be adjusted at will. The following figure employs longer tic marks than we have seen so far:

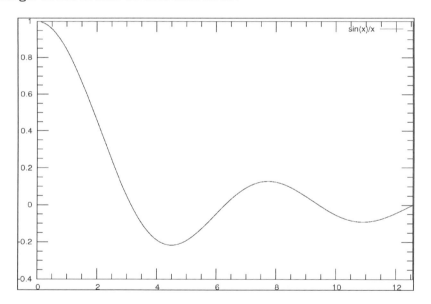

How to do it...

Following is an example showing how to specify the length of the tic marks. The output of this script is the previous figure:

```
set tics scale 3
set mxtics 4
set mytics 4
plot [0:4*pi] sin(x)/x
```

How it works...

The first (highlighted) code line sets the length of the tic marks to be three times the default length. The actual length may vary somewhat between terminals, so you may need to experiment to get the exact effect that you desire.

There's more...

By default, gnuplot assigns a length to the minor tics that is one-half the length of the major tics, so in this case the minor tics have a scale of 1.5. If you want to set a different scale for the minor tics, the command becomes set tics scale a, b, where a is the scale for the major tics and b is the scale for the minor tics. You may even make the minor tics longer than the major tics if, for some reason, you want to.

Removing all tics

Here is one way to remove the tics entirely from the plot. This gives a clean and simple appearance for applications where you need an illustration and the reader is not expected to glean quantitative information from the graph.

How to do it...

A ticless graph is accomplished very simply. The following script produces the figure
following it:

```
unset tics
plot [0:2*pi] x**2*sin(x)
```

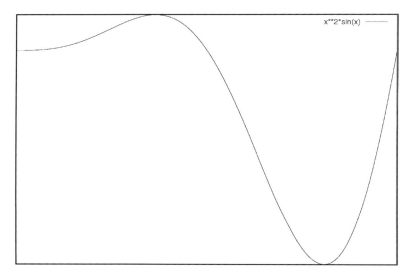

How it works...

The highlighted line simply tells gnuplot to not draw tics; we still get a border around the plot,
but no tic marks, and consequently, no numerical labels on the axes.

Defining the tic values

This recipe will show you how to take a little more control over where the tics appear on your axes. The following figure illustrates one use of manually specified tic marks:

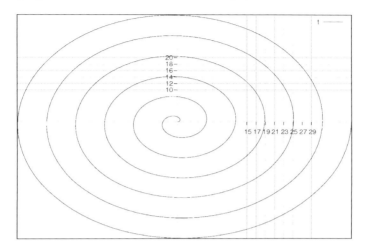

The previous figure is similar to the one towards the end of *Chapter 1, Plotting Curves, Boxes, Points, and more*, where we introduced polar coordinates. The difference here is that we have placed our tic marks only in a certain area—that you can imagine is a region of interest—and added grid lines so the reader can more easily extract quantitative information from the graph in the region.

How to do it...

Following is the script that produced the previous figure:

```
set xtics axis nomirror
set ytics axis nomirror
set zeroaxis
unset border
set polar
set samples 500
set grid
set xtics 15,2,30
set ytics 10,2,20
plot [0:12*pi] t
```

How it works...

The lines in the previous script until the highlighted lines are the same as in the *Plotting with polar coordinates* recipe towards the end of *Chapter 1, Plotting Curves, Boxes, Points, and more*. The new commands here set the beginning, interval, and ending values for the tics on the x and y axes. The x-axis will only have tic marks, and associated numerical labels, starting at x=15 and ending at x=30, and marks will be drawn at intervals of 2 on the x-axis (so the highest valued tic mark is actually at x=29). The y-axis will have tic marks going from 10 to 20 at intervals of 2.

Making the tics stick out

The following figure illustrates another tic style available in gnuplot, where the tics stick out of the plot rather than intrude on the interior of the graph:

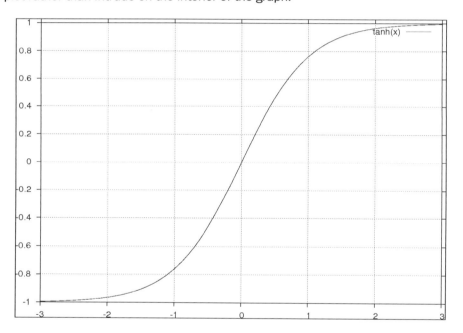

This style is useful when inner tic marks might obscure your plot elements, for example, when part of the curve lies close to an axis.

How to do it...

Following is the script used to obtain the previous figure:

```
set tics out
set grid
plot [-3:3] tanh(x)
```

How it works...

The new command here is the first line, which leaves everything else the same while drawing the tics so that they stick out of the borders.

Setting manual tics

Sometimes gnuplot's various automatic tic generation routines are not flexible enough and you need to take complete control of the position of every tic mark, or you need to place custom labels on the tics rather than rely on the automatically generated numerical labels provided by the program. gnuplot is extremely flexible in this regard; the following figure illustrates our first example of manual tic placement:

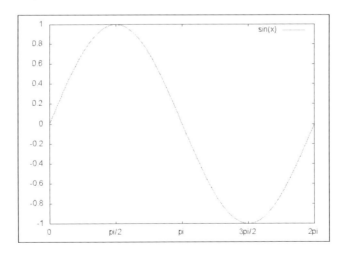

Notice the tic labels and positions along the x-axis. The tics are aligned with the peaks and zero crossings of the sine wave, and are labeled using **pi** rather than an approximate decimal. This is more meaningful mathematically and is the natural way to label the axis when plotting this circular function. gnuplot's automatically chosen tic positions and numerical labels would be placed at the positions 1, 2, 3, and so on. These tic positions would have no particular relation to the function we are plotting. In order to get the result in the figure, we need to specify each tic and associated label manually.

How to do it...

The following script illustrates the creation of manual tic marks. This script produced the previous figure:

```
set xtics \
  ("pi" pi, "pi/2" pi/2, "2pi" 2*pi, "3pi/2" 3*pi/2, "0" 0)
plot [0:2*pi] sin(x)
```

How it works...

The highlighted line shows the syntax for setting manual tics and labels. Here, we're setting the tics on the *x*-axis; the list of manual tic positions is enclosed in parentheses. The label for each tic is the string in double quotation marks. Following the label is the position for the tic on the axis, which is given in units of *pi*. Since gnuplot knows what *pi* means, we can use the constant directly rather than needing to spell it out as a decimal approximation. Note that the tics can be given in any order. The textual labels can be omitted, allowing you to specify an arbitrary set of tics, which will automatically be given numerical labels.

There's more...

The following figure is almost the same as the previous one, except for the labels on the *x*-axis tic marks:

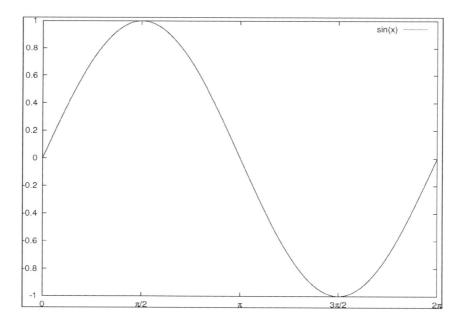

Note the appearance of Greek letters in the tic labels, where before we spelled out *pi*. We constructed these labels using the enhanced text syntax that was introduced in *Chapter 2, Annotating with Labels and Legends* as shown in the following script:

```
set term wxt enhanced
set xtics ("{/Symbol p}" pi, "{/Symbol p}/2" pi/2,\
    "2{/Symbol p}" 2*pi, "3{/Symbol p}/2" 3*pi/2, "0" 0)
plot [0:2*pi] sin(x)
```

For this to work, we must use a terminal that supports enhanced text, and turn on the option in the `set term` line. If you are using a terminal that supports Unicode text, you may be able to use Unicode characters directly in the tic specifications rather than the relatively cumbersome enhanced text syntax.

You can combine a regular, automatically generated set of tics with another set that you specify manually, as mentioned earlier, by using the keyword `add`. Instead of the `set xtics` line in the previous script, you can use the following command:

```
set xtics add ("{/Symbol p}" pi, "2{/Symbol p}" 2*pi)
```

You get the automatic tics that gnuplot would provide in any case, with the addition of the extra tics that you specify manually. This is useful to call attention to a small number of salient coordinate positions; here we have shown the locations of π and 2π on the axis, where the sine wave crosses y = 0. The following figure shows the use of add with `xtics`:

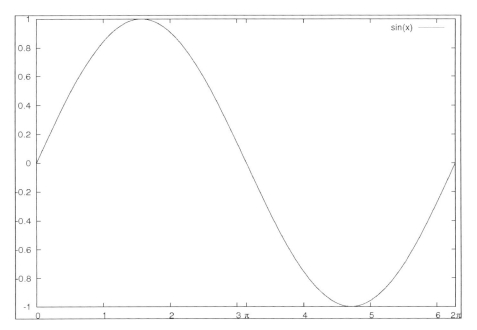

Plotting with dates and times

gnuplot is capable of handling data plotted along a date/time axis and can understand and display dates and times in a variety of formats.

Getting ready

If you are plotting data versus time, you are almost certainly dealing with data tabulated in a file. We have supplied a small file for this recipe called `timedat.dat`; it consists of a few lines of data, each line containing a date, time, and a number to be plotted. The dates are in the form day/month/2-digit-year, and the times are in the form hour:minute. Following is the first line:

```
1/1/11 19:00 72.01
```

The following figure shows plotting with dates using gnuplot:

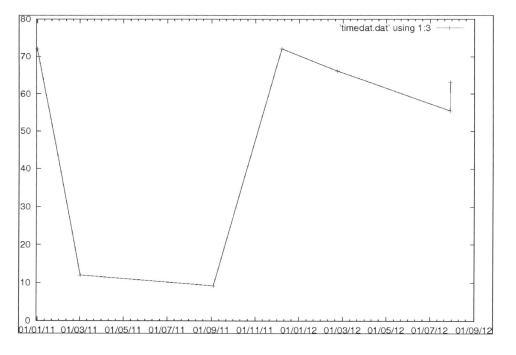

Note that the tics along the bottom axis are labeled as dates.

How to do it...

Following is the script that we used to get the previous figure:

```
set xdata time
set timefmt "%d/%m/%y %H:%M"
set format x "%d/%m/%y"
plot 'timedat.dat' using 1:3 with linespoints
```

How it works...

When dealing with date/time data, you must always alert gnuplot to this with `set xdata time`. Then you need to tell the program in what format the date and time data will be found; this is the purpose of the `set timefmt` command. The format string uses `%d` to stand for the numerical day, `%H` to stand for the numerical hour using a 24-hour clock, and so on. For a rundown of all the formats that gnuplot understands, type `help timefmt` at the interactive prompt.

The third line sets the format for the tic labels on the *x*-axis (which is now a date/time axis). The final line plots the file; the `using` keyword is mandatory when plotting temporal data.

If you want you can put the time of day in the tic labels as well (and you must if your data lies within one day, for example). Try using the following command:

```
set format x "%d/%m/%y\n%H:%M"
```

This will get you the date as formatted in the previous figure with the time set below each date. The escape code `\n` in the format specification produces a new line in the label, which puts the time of day below the date.

The use of dates and times in tic labels can take up a lot of horizontal space. gnuplot does a poor job of accounting for space used in tic labels. So, in such situations, we often need to take measures to keep the labels from running into each other. The use of a linebreak embedded in the tic format is one remedy. It may also help to change the font.

Changing the language used for labels [new]

The most recent version of gnuplot provides several new internationalization features. If you are plotting date/time data and set the format to display the month abbreviation rather than the number of the month, gnuplot can use the abbreviations appropriate to any language installed on your system. The following figure repeats the previous plot using month abbreviations and the Spanish language:

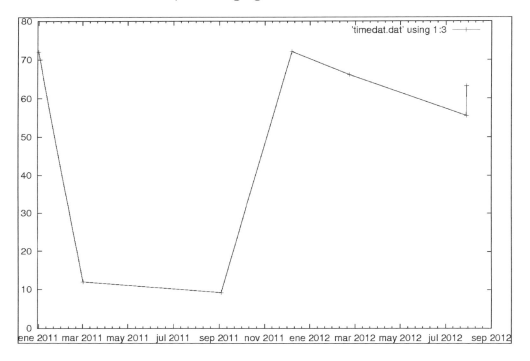

Note that the month names are not capitalized, which is the convention in Spanish.

How to do it...

In the following script, the addition of one line translates our plot to Spanish:

```
set xdata time
set locale "es_ES.utf8"
set timefmt "%d/%m/%y %H:%M"
set format x "%b %Y"
plot 'timedat.dat' using 1:3 with linespoints
```

How it works...

In order to use the new internationalization features, you must have the `locale` program installed on your system; how this is handled is highly system dependent. In Linux, you install the desired language packages, and get a list of the available locales at the system command line with `locale -a`. You can switch languages in gnuplot with the `set locale` command highlighted in the previous script, substituting a locale name from the available list. gnuplot should be able to detect the default language of your system, so if you want to create labels using your computer's native language, you will most likely need to do nothing. In the `set format x` line in the previous script we've used the symbols for the month abbreviation (`%b`) and for the full, four-digit year (`%Y`).

Using European-style decimals [new]

Another new internationalization feature in gnuplot 4.4 is the ability to set the character used for the decimal point to be correct for the `locale` in use. In most European countries the comma is used, whereas in the U.S. the period is conventional.

How to do it...

The following script produces the graph that follows it:

```
set decimalsign locale "es_ES.utf8"
plot [0:1] x**3
```

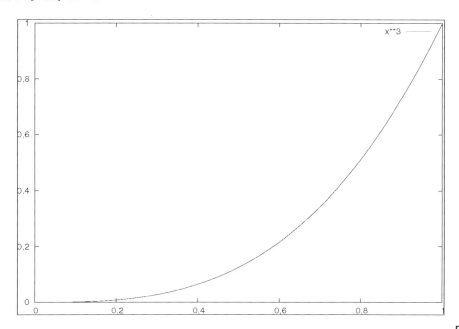

Note that the periods used for decimal points that we've seen in all the examples until now have become commas, because gnuplot knows that that is the convention when using the Spanish language.

How it works...

The new command `set decimalsign` selects the correct decimal separator for the `locale` specified. We can also select any symbol here explicitly. If we would like a vertical bar to stand in for the decimal point, for example, we can say `set decimalsign "|"`. These customizations only affect the output on the graph.

Changing the `decimalsign` does not change what gnuplot will be expecting when it reads your input data.

Formatting tic labels

gnuplot provides a great deal of flexibility in the formatting of numbers in tic labels and allows us to freely intermix text with its automatically generated numbers. This is illustrated in the following figure:

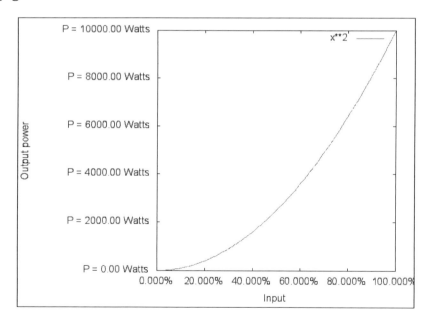

How to do it...

The following script introduces the formatting commands that we used to produce the previous figure:

```
set ylabel "Output power"
set format y "P = %.2f Watts"
set format x "%.3f%%"
set rmargin 6
plot [0:100] x**2
```

How it works...

The new commands are in the highlighted lines. `set format y` and `set format x` define the formats to be used for the tic labels on the *y* and *x*-axes, respectively. For a complete rundown of all the options, you can type `help set format` at the gnuplot interactive prompt. Here, we shall describe the subset of the formatting language that we used in the script. The codes are very similar to those used in many programming languages for the output formatting of numbers.

A formatting specification is introduced by the character `%`. It contains a letter that determines in what general form the number should be represented. We use `f`, which means "floating point", which is a simple number with a decimal point. Other options include exponential ("scientific") notation. The notation between the `%` and `f` that has the form `.n` means to use `n` places after the decimal point.

Everything before the initial `%` and after the format specifier (`f`) is a string that is copied verbatim. Since `%` has a special meaning, it is escaped by doubling it to express a percentage in the tic labels.

As mentioned earlier, gnuplot does not generally do a good job of accounting for the horizontal space used by big tic labels, as in the example, where the use of three places after the decimal point makes our labels fairly long. The problem this leads to in the previous figure is that the last tic label on the *x*-axis will be cut off on the right. This is fixed by the line after the two highlighted format lines, where the `rmargin` setting increases the size of the right margin, using character coordinates.

There's more...

What if we want tics with no labels on them at all? The following figure has tic marks but no labels:

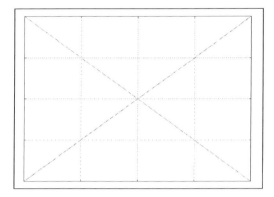

All we need to do in this case is to specify empty formats for the tic labels, as follows:

```
set format y ""
set format x ""
unset key
set grid
plot x, -x
```

5
Combining Multiple Plots

This chapter contains the following recipes:

- ▶ Arranging an array of plots
- ▶ Positioning plots manually
- ▶ Creating an inset plot
- ▶ Multiplotting with labels and arrows

Introduction

This chapter will show you how to combine several plots into a larger visualization using gnuplot's **multiplot** mode. This is a flexible facility that allows you to place a set of plots anywhere on the page, in a regular array, or one inside the other.

Arranging an array of plots

The simplest use of the multiplot mode creates a rectangular array of plots with regular spacing. The following figure is an example of this type of multiple plot:

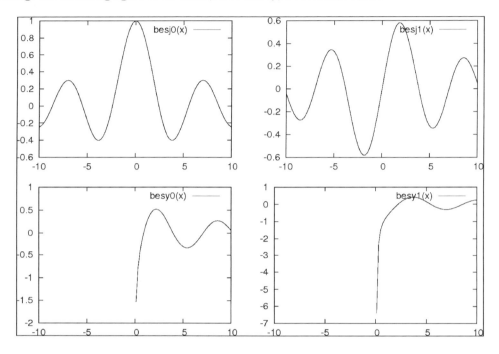

In the previous figure, we have made a table of graphs showing the four kinds of Bessel function that gnuplot has built in.

How to do it...

Run this script through gnuplot to get the array of plots shown in the previous figure:

```
set multiplot layout 2, 2
plot besj0(x)
plot besj1(x)
plot besy0(x)
plot besy1(x)
unset multiplot
```

How it works...

The new command is in the first line of the recipe. The commands following that are simple plot statements, until we reach the final line. The initial command puts gnuplot into **multiplot mode**. If you are working interactively, you will see that the prompt, which is usually `gnuplot>`, has become `multiplot>` to remind you that you are in a special mode.

The `layout 2, 2` part of the command sets up a regular array of plots with two columns and two rows; of course you can use any numbers here. The subsequent plot commands will fill the places in this array from left to right and top to bottom.

The final `unset multiplot` command returns to normal gnuplot mode. In some terminals, nothing is displayed or written to a file until this command is issued; in others, the page is built up as you enter the plot commands.

Positioning plots manually

If you need an arrangement of figures other than a regular rectangular array, you must specify the origin and size for each plot manually. The following figure provides an example:

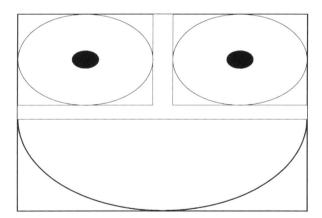

The happy face shown in the previous figure is a simple example of what you can achieve with manual plot positioning; using these commands, figures of frightening complexity can be built up.

How to do it...

The following script shows how to use gnuplot's manual positioning commands:

```
set multiplot
unset key
unset tics
set polar
set size 1, .5
plot [pi:2*pi] 1 lw 5
set origin 0, .5
set size .5, .5
plot 1 lw 2, .2 with filledcurves
set origin .5, .5
plot 1 lw 2, .2 with filledcurves
unset multiplot
```

How it works...

Arbitrary sizing and positioning of individual plots is accomplished using the two new commands that we have highlighted in the previous script. After entering `multiplot` mode, the `set origin` command can be used to set the position of the lower-left corner of the next plot. The `set size` command sets the size of the plot. Both commands use screen coordinates (since there are no coordinate axes to define any other coordinate system) and are passed the *x* and *y* coordinates separated by a comma. Unlike the situation when we are using the automatic graph positioning facility introduced in the previous recipe, the order in which we draw the individual plots does not matter, since the absolute position of each one is specified separately. The other commands in the script are familiar from previous recipes; the key and tics were done away with to create a simple, clean figure, and polar coordinates were used to allow us to easily draw circles.

There's more...

Note that, although we have selected origins and sizes that place the plots touching each other, there seems to be some space between them. This is because gnuplot by default places a margin around each plot, and the command `set origin` establishes the location of the lower-left corner of the plot including the invisible margin. If we want our plots to be closer together, farther apart, or we would like to adjust the spacing differently in different directions, we must turn to the commands that set the individual margins. These are `set bmargin` for the bottom margin, `set lmargin` for the left margin, and so on. (All four margin commands make an appearance in the next recipe.) The coordinate system used in setting these lengths is neither the screen system nor an axis system, but yet another gnuplot coordinate system, the **character coordinate system**. This is based on the size of a character in the currently chosen font. The use of this coordinate system for margins is rather convenient, as it allows us to relate the thickness of a margin to the size of the tic labels by counting characters.

Creating an inset plot

A common pattern is a graph enclosing another smaller graph that reveals a detail in the larger graph by plotting it using a magnified scale. Following is an example:

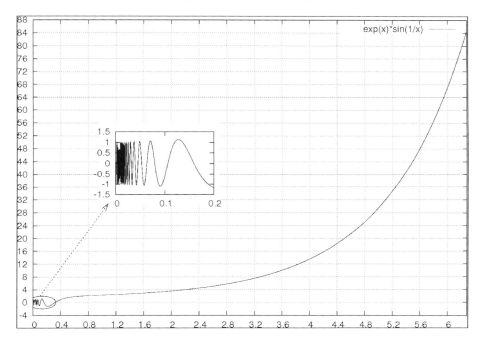

In the previous figure, the smaller plot is usually called an **inset**. We can create this figure with the script given in the following *How to do it...* section.

How to do it...

The following script produces the previous figure:

```
set multiplot
set object ellipse center .13, 0 size .4, 4
set arrow from .1, 2.1 to screen .22, .4 front lt 3
set samples 1000
set grid
set xtics .4
set ytics 4
plot [0:2*pi] exp(x)*sin(1/x)
set origin .2, .4
set size .25,.25
```

```
clear
unset key
unset grid
unset object
unset arrow
set xtics .1
set ytics .5
set bmargin 1
set tmargin 1
set lmargin 3
set rmargin 1
plot [0:.2] exp(x)*sin(1/x)
unset multiplot
```

How it works...

There are few new commands here. We have simply combined several things covered earlier in order to create an illustration consisting of a large graph, an inset, and a device consisting of an oval surrounding a region of interest and an arrow pointing to the inset, indicating that the latter is a magnification of the region.

After entering multiplot mode, we define an ellipse object (see *Chapter 3, Applying Colors and Styles* for an introduction to the use of objects, where we used circle objects in order to construct a pie chart). The ellipse's center and size are given as (*x,y*) pairs in the default axis coordinates. This defines a shape that will not be drawn immediately but deferred to the next plot command. The next line defines the arrow. This is a good example of when it can be convenient to mix axis and screen coordinates, and illustrates the utility of gnuplot's several coordinate systems. We want the origin of the arrow to touch the ellipse; the required (*x,y*) location is most easily read directly from the graph, suggesting the use of the axis ("first") coordinate system. This is the default, so it need not be specified explicitly. We want the destination of the arrow to point at where we will eventually place our inset, and that is specified in screen coordinates, which are useful for eyeballing the illustration and estimating where a pleasing location for the inset graph might be. The keyword **front** in the arrow specification tells gnuplot to draw the arrow on top of any other graph elements that it might intersect.

The first plot command in the script uses the entire screen by default. After that we issue `origin` and `size` commands for the inset. The next command, `clear`, erases anything on the plot in the area defined by the most recent `origin` and `size` commands. The purpose of this is to erase the grid lines in the area that will be used for the inset, as they will not align with the latter's tic marks and would be confusing.

Before drawing the inset graph, we unset the grid and key in order to make the smaller graph less busy. We also unset the ellipse object and the arrow so that they are not drawn again with the next plot command, and reduce the frequency of tic marks. In addition, we adjust the size of the margins (see the *There's more...* section of the *Positioning plots manually* recipe in this chapter); in particular, the bottom margin is reduced so that the arrowhead lies closer to the inset graph axes.

Finally, we create our inset graph by plotting the same function over a smaller interval.

Multiplotting with labels and arrows

In this recipe, we show how to create a complete illustration that might be useful in a calculus textbook, using arrows and the `screen` coordinate system to lead the eye around a cycle of graphs. The following figure shows what happens when we take successive derivatives of a sine wave:

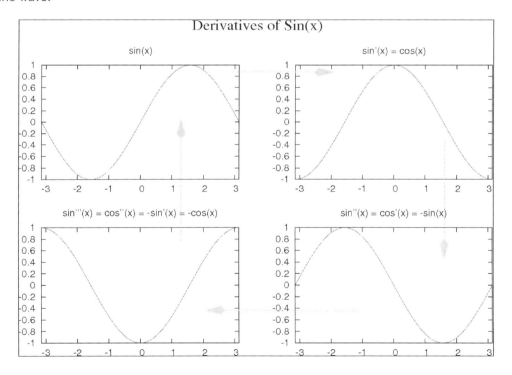

How to do it...

The following script will give you the previous figure:

```
set xrange [-pi:pi]
unset key
set multiplot layout 2,2 title "Derivatives of Sin(x)" font "Times-
Roman, 22"
set style arrow 1 head filled size screen 0.03,15,135 lt 2 lw 2
set arrow 1 from screen .45, .84 to screen .65, .84 arrowstyle 1
set arrow 2 from screen .87, .64 to screen .87, .3 arrowstyle 1
set arrow 3 from screen .7, .15 to screen .4, .15 arrowstyle 1
set arrow 4 from screen .35, .35 to screen .35, .7 arrowstyle 1
set title "sin(x)"
plot sin(x)
set title "sin\'(x) = cos(x)"
plot cos(x)
set title "sin\'\'\'(x) = cos\'\'(x) = -sin\'(x) = -cos(x)"
plot -cos(x)
set title "sin\'\'(x) = cos\'(x) = -sin(x)"
plot -sin(x)
unset multiplot
```

How it works...

Since we want each plot in the set to have the same range on the x-axis, we'll save typing by defining the **xrange** first. The highlighted `set multiplot` line has some features we've not covered earlier. The title here will be the overall title for the entire illustration, rather than for any individual plot. We would like it to be more prominent than the rest of the text on the page, so we use a font specifier here as well.

The next command (the second highlighted line) defines a user style for an arrow, similar to the user-defined linestyles we covered in *Chapter 3, Applying Colors and Styles*. As we'll use this same style for the four arrows pointing between the graphs, it's more economical to define a user style rather than repeating the style information for each arrow command. `head filled` means to draw a solid arrowhead; the numbers following the `screen` coordinate selector define the length of the arrowhead, the angle its front sides make with the shaft, and the angle of its back sides. gnuplot provides maximum flexibility in the drawing of arrowheads. Once the style is defined, we use it in the next four `set arrow` commands, selecting the style with the invocation `arrowstyle 1` (which, like most gnuplot keywords, can be severely abbreviated, in this case to `as`).

Now, each `set title` command defines the title for the individual plot that follows it, and the four plots with their titles are arranged in a 2 x 2 array that was defined in the `set multiplot` command.

6
Including Plots in Documents

This chapter contains the following recipes:

- ▶ Introducing gnuplot's high-quality graphics formats [new]
- ▶ Adding a plot to a paper using LaTeX
- ▶ Assembling a document using TikZ and LaTeX [new]
- ▶ Assembling a document using epslatex
- ▶ Using gnuplot within LaTeX
- ▶ Creating presentation slides with incrementally displayed graphs
- ▶ Including a plot in a web page
- ▶ Making an interactive plot for the Web [new]

Introduction

The previous chapters have all dealt with the creation of graphs, or of illustrations made up of sets of graphs, as isolated files or images on the screen. But in the real world, graphs and charts are often not content to stand on their own. The lucky ones become part of something larger. In this chapter, you will learn various techniques that will allow you to include your plots in technical documents, presentations, and web pages. The emphasis throughout will be on using the special capabilities of gnuplot, including some of its most recently added features, that allow it to work in close cooperation with document creation software for the production of the highest quality typeset or interactive documents.

The nature of what we shall be learning in this chapter means that there is an important difference between it and the previous ones. Up to now all you needed to follow the recipes in this book was a working installation of gnuplot and perhaps some auxiliary programs such as text editors and viewers for graphical files. But for some of the recipes in this chapter you will need to have installed some additional non-trivial software and have some knowledge of how to use it. This cannot be avoided, because we are concerned here with the creation of documents, and this is something that gnuplot does not do by itself. For the recipes where we show you how to create documents for the Web, however, all you will need besides a text editor is a modern graphical web browser.

Introducing gnuplot's high-quality graphics formats [new]

The `pdf` and `png` terminal drivers have been supplemented (or perhaps replaced, depending on the details of how your version of gnuplot was compiled) by higher quality versions that use the **cairo** graphics library.

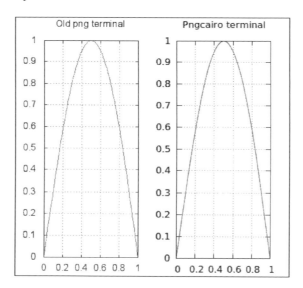

As the emphasis in this chapter is on achieving the highest possible quality for publication in electronic documents or on paper, we are devoting the first recipe to showing you how to select and use gnuplot's new high-quality terminal drivers.

In the previous figure, we can clearly see the increase in quality when using the new `pngcairo` terminal driver rather than the older, libgd-based terminal. Text and anti-aliasing is handled better, and the drawing of curves in plots is vastly improved. The curve in the older version is clearly more jagged, while the cairo library smoothly interpolates the curve between sample points.

Getting ready

To reproduce this recipe, your version of gnuplot needs to have the `pngcairo` terminal compiled in. You can check this by typing `set term` at the gnuplot prompt to get a list of all the available output devices. The terminals you can use depend not merely on the version of gnuplot that you have, but on the details of how it was compiled. If by chance you have the `pdfcairo` terminal but not `pngcairo`, you can use the former and create a PNG file using, for example, Ghostscript.

How to do it...

Try the following script to produce the right-hand side of the figure:

```
set term pngcairo
set title 'Pngcairo terminal'
set out 'file.png'
unset key
set grid
set size .4,1
plot [0:1] sin(pi*x)
```

If you run this script at the system command line with `gnuplot scriptname`, then `file.png` should appear in your current directory. If you enter or load it at gnuplot's interactive prompt, the file will not be complete until you exit gnuplot normally or enter a new `set out` command.

How it works...

In the highlighted code line, we have selected the `pngcairo` terminal driver.

We've set the `size` to be thinner than normal, so that we could conveniently display the output of this script next to the output of the same script when replacing the first line with `set term png`, which selects the older version of the png terminal. The difference in quality is so great that there is no reason to use the latter any more if you have the cairo terminal drivers installed. If you need to create a bitmapped graphics file (for subsequent editing or because of the needs of your workflow) then the `pngcairo` terminal is probably the best choice. PNG is also a great choice for use on web pages, as it is supported in the recent versions of all graphical browsers and gives far better results than jpeg for the type of graphics that we create with gnuplot. Yet another advantage of the new `pngcairo` terminal is that it fully supports the new gnuplot features **transparency** (covered in *Chapter 3, Applying Colors and Styles*) and **Unicode** (covered in *Chapter 2, Annotating with Labels and Legends*), neither of which are handled by the libgd-based png terminal.

There's more...

There are some other recent additions to gnuplot's collection of output devices, which include the following terminals:

The wxt terminal

Another addition to the gnuplot stable is the wxt terminal, which is an interactive bitmapped display similar in use to the venerable X11 terminal. The improvements here are that the wxt terminal uses the cairo graphics library, and thus also features sophisticated font handling, including Unicode, smooth curve drawing, and anti-aliasing. The wxt terminal supports transparency as well, which the X11 terminal does not. The wxt driver also puts several interactive widgets on the screen that allow you to turn the grid on or off, set some basic configuration, flip through your zoom levels, and copy the image to the clipboard. All of these except the last are also available as keyboard shortcuts (type *h* while the graphics window is in focus to get a list of these shortcuts printed on the console), as they are in the X11 terminal as well. The copy-to-clipboard function is especially useful here, as it allows you to conveniently transfer a high-quality bitmapped image to a graphics program for further editing after adjusting it interactively. This can also be a convenient way to insert graphs in word processor documents, although better quality will be obtained by saving your graph in a vector format (see the next paragraph) and inserting the external file (many widely used word processors can include PDF or SVG files, either built-in or through plugins), and for the best quality and convenience of automation you will want to use the LaTeX methods described later. In short, there is little reason to use the old X11 terminal if the wxt driver is available on your installation, and in fact it has replaced the former as the default starting terminal out of the box. There is one reason why you might want to switch to using the X11 terminal in some situations, however, and that is because interactive scaling and rotation can be a bit slower in wxt for complex 3D graphs, depending on your hardware. To invoke the wxt terminal, just use the command `set term wxt`.

The pdfcairo terminal

If you do not need to produce a bitmapped file, you will get superior results by saving your graphs in a vector format. These graphical formats are resolution-independent, meaning that they can be scaled up arbitrarily without loss of quality. They consist of drawing and character-placement instructions rather than the list of colored dots comprising a bitmapped format.

New in version 4.4 of gnuplot is the `pdfcairo` terminal. As the name suggests, this driver produces a PDF file that uses the `cairo` graphics library. The results are superior to the older driver based on the `PDFLib` library, and `pdfcairo` supports gnuplot's new transparency and Unicode features as well. This is important because PostScript supports neither transparency, nor, generally, Unicode, so a PDF made by transforming a PostScript file (a common workflow) cannot have these features. The pdfcairo terminal should probably be your first choice for producing high-quality, standalone files for printing or inclusion in typeset documents. To set the terminal type `set term pdfcairo` on the gnuplot command prompt.

The svg terminal

Another relatively recent addition to gnuplot's device lineup is the SVG terminal. This is another high-quality vector format that also supports transparency and Unicode; it produces very attractive plots. The chief value of SVG is that it is a vector format that can be included directly in web pages; indeed it was developed by the W3C for this purpose. If you are producing graphs for use on the Web, the SVG terminal is your best choice, unless you need to support very old browsers. It will probably come as no surprise that to select this driver you type `set term svg`.

Adding a plot to a paper using LaTeX

As promised in the Introduction to this chapter, here is a recipe where you will need more than gnuplot to carry it out. This example assumes that you have a working LaTeX installation, including several common packages. For most people using gnuplot in the production of scientific or technical documents, this is a fairly safe assumption, as LaTeX is the preeminent platform for demanding technical typesetting. If you do not have LaTeX available or are unfamiliar with its workings, then this section might serve as an advertisement and, along with the next several recipes, provide a survey of what you can do when you get LaTeX and gnuplot working together. In the following figure, we have a section of what might be a gnuplot tutorial, showing a paragraph of text and a graph:

It can be difficult to plot functions like $\sin(\frac{1}{x})$ that vary infinitely quickly as x approaches a particular value, in this case $x = 0$. Unless the function is sampled more frequently than it oscillates, you will

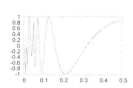

produce plotting artifacts, as can be seen in the figure to the right. In these cases a better result can be obtained by increasing the sample frequency; in gnuplot the command is **set samples 1000**, for example.

The graph was produced by gnuplot and saved in its own file. Then a LaTeX document was created that referenced this file and put it together with the typeset paragraph. Therefore, we have two code samples: the usual gnuplot script, which we list first, and the LaTeX source document, which we list after that in its entirety.

Getting ready

Make sure that you have a working installation of LaTeX, that the `pdflatex` command works, and that you can view the resulting `pdf` files.

On Linux, the simplest way to install the LaTeX system will be to use your package manager: look for a package called `texlive`. On other systems you can visit the official web page at `http://www.tug.org/texlive/acquire-netinstall.html`.

How to do it...

Following are the steps to produce the previous figure:

Creating the figure

First, enter the following script and create your figure with gnuplot:

```
set term pdfcairo font "Arial,12"
set out 'r2fig.pdf'
unset key
plot [0:.5] sin(1/x) lw 2
```

The TeX document

Next, create a document with the following content and save it with the filename `r2.tex`:

```
\documentclass[12pt]{article}
\usepackage[rflt]{floatflt}
\usepackage{graphicx}
\pagestyle{empty}
\begin{document}
\openup.5em
\begin{floatingfigure}{2.25in}
\includegraphics[width=2in]{r2fig}
\end{floatingfigure}
It can be difficult to plot functions like $\sin(\frac{1}{x})$ that
vary infinitely quickly as $x$ approaches a particular value, in this
case $x=0$. Unless the function is sampled more frequently than it
oscillates, you will produce plotting artifacts, as can be seen in
the figure to the right. In
these cases a better result can be obtained by increasing the sample
frequency; in gnuplot the command is {\tt set samples 1000}, for
example.
\end{document}
```

Running LaTeX

Now, after making sure that you are in a directory with both the `r2.tex` file and the `r2fig.pdf` file, issue the command `pdflatex r2` in the terminal (the console, or wherever you issue commands in your shell). If you are using a graphical interface to LaTeX, such as TeXshop on the Macintosh, that should work just as well and produce identical results, as these programs simply call the command given here behind the scenes. If all goes well, after LaTeX finishes digesting your file you should have a new file called `r2.pdf` in your directory (as well as `r2.aux` and others that we can ignore for now). This file should be essentially identical to the previous figure.

How it works...

The gnuplot part of the recipe should all be pretty familiar. We have chosen to save our graph in the form of a PDF because our final document will also be a PDF, and we want all of its components to be resolution independent and able to be printed or displayed at the highest quality. Since the default font size for this terminal is quite small, we've selected a larger size so that the tic labels will be more visible and will more closely match the document text.

In the plot command, we have specified a line width larger than the default (`lw 2`). This is a good idea for plots that may be reduced in size for publication or inclusion in a document, as this one is, because the default thin lines usually produced by gnuplot may become almost invisible when the entire plot is reduced.

After we run the gnuplot script and have the graph stored on disc, we process the LaTeX file, which will look for the graph when `pdflatex` hits the highlighted `\includegraphics` line. Note that we just include the base name of the graphics file, without the `.pdf` extension; LaTeX knows how to look for graphics files that it can handle, and tries the extensions that it knows about until it finds an appropriate file. This is generally better practice than specifying the full filename, as it makes it convenient to substitute a different format later if you change your mind.

The line `\usepackage[rflt]{floatflt}` loads a package that defines the `floatingfigure` environment, within which we have inserted our `\includegraphics` command. This environment floats the figure to the side (the right side in this case, because of the `[rflt]` option) and the nearby text flows around it.

Assembling a document using TikZ and LaTeX [new]

The previous recipe showed how to add a gnuplot graph to a LaTeX document by saving the graph in a file and including it with an `\includegraphics` command. There is nothing in this method that requires the illustration to be a graph produced with gnuplot; any graphics format that is understood by the version of LaTeX (pdflatex, regular LaTeX, or something else) that you are running can be used. That makes this method particularly useful when you need to save a bitmapped version of your graph so that you can edit it to produce a final version in an image editing program (Gimp, Photoshop, and so on).

However, there are drawbacks to this approach. Ideally, you would like the fonts used in your graph, in the tic labels, title, and elsewhere, to match the fonts used in the rest of your document. This produces a unified, sophisticated appearance, and increases overall legibility. It is quite difficult to do this entirely within gnuplot, or in an image editor. Even if you could get these programs to find and use the fonts that will be used by LaTeX in typesetting your document, there would be no way to match the typographic detail incorporated by LaTeX in the main text: the kerning, linebreaking, ligatures, and so on. And when you need to include an equation in your graph, you would not have access to TeX's mathematical syntax nor any way to produce results comparable to TeX's math output. Your best alternative would be to use the *enhanced text* markup we covered in *Chapter 2, Annotating with Labels and Legends*, which is cumbersome, unpredictable, and usually leads to unattractive results (but can be convenient in simple cases).

This recipe shows how to use a new feature in gnuplot version **4.4** to overcome all these problems and get LaTeX to produce all of the text on your graph. You have full access to the entire power of LaTeX for mathematical typesetting and all the features of gnuplot at the same time. The result is a vector drawing seamlessly incorporated into your document, as can be seen in the following figure:

The figure to the right pro-vides an illustration of L'Hô-pital's Rule. Recall that this rule can be applied when taking the limit as $x \longrightarrow x_a$ of a ratio of two functions where the ratio approaches the indeterminate form $\frac{0}{0}$; in the case where both functions are

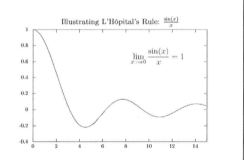

differentiable at x_a, the ratio approaches the ratio of their derivatives. In the case illustrated both $\sin(x)$ and $x \longrightarrow 0$ as we approach the origin, but the ratio of their derivatives, $\frac{\cos(x)}{1} \longrightarrow 1$. L'Hôpital's Rule also applies in the case of the indeterminate form $\frac{\infty}{\infty}$.

In the previous figure, we have what might be an extract from an elementary calculus textbook. You might notice three things: the typefaces used in the graph, including the numbers used as tic labels, are identical with those used in the text; the kerning used in the title reflects the same high-quality typesetting seen elsewhere on the page; and the mathematical material looks like real math. The overall effect is that of a professionally typeset book. This is surprisingly easy to achieve, thanks to gnuplot's built-in mechanisms for working with LaTeX.

Getting ready

As in the previous recipe, you need to have a relatively recent installation of LaTeX. Also, the `tikz` terminal needs to have been compiled into your version of gnuplot.

How to do it...

Follow these steps to create the previous figure:

Making the plot

As in the previous recipe, there are two pieces of code required. First, the gnuplot script:

```
set terminal tikz
set out 'r3.tex'
unset key
set label '\Large$\displaystyle \lim_{x\Longrightarrow0}\frac{\sin(x)}
{x}=1$' at graph .55, .75
set title '\Large Illustrating L'H\^opital's Rule: $\frac{\sin(x)}
{x}$'
plot [0:15] sin(x)/x lw 2
```

The first (highlighted) line invokes the `tikz` terminal, which is new in gnuplot version 4.4. The final result of running this through gnuplot will not be a graphics file, such as a PDF or PNG image, but a tex file, consisting of a set of instructions for LaTeX that you can (but need not) read and edit in a text editor. The file is named in the second line; you can call it anything, but it will be convenient to name it with the `tex` extension. The `set label` and `set title` commands are familiar from previous chapters, but here we have used LaTeX syntax in the strings. You can use almost anything that you can use in the main part of your LaTeX document here, with one big exception: the display math delimiters or environment do not work. That is why, in the label definition, we've used the `\displaystyle` command; this makes the rest of the equation typeset as if it were in a displayed equation environment.

 You cannot use displayed math environments directly with the `tikz` terminal.

The LaTeX document

After running the previous script through gnuplot, if you have the `tikz` terminal installed, you should have the new file `r3.tex` ready to be included in your main document. The following listing shows the LaTeX file that produced the previous figure:

```
\documentclass{article}
\usepackage{graphicx}
\usepackage[rflt]{floatflt}
```

```
\usepackage[T1]{fontenc}
\usepackage{textcomp}
\usepackage[utf8x]{inputenc}
\usepackage{gnuplot-lua-tikz}
\pagestyle{empty}
\begin{document}
\openup.5em
\begin{floatingfigure}{2.9in}
\resizebox{2.5in}{!}{\input{r3}}
\end{floatingfigure}
\noindent The figure to the right provides an illustration of
L'H\^o\-pi\-tal's Rule.  Recall that this rule can be applied when
taking the limit as $x\longrightarrow x_a$ of a ratio of two
functions where the ratio approaches the indeterminate form
$\frac{0}{0}$; in the case where both functions are
differentiable at $x_a$, the ratio approaches the ratio of their
derivatives. In the case illustrated both $\sin(x)$ and $x
\longrightarrow0$ as we approach the origin, but the ratio of their
derivatives, $\frac{\cos(x)}{1} \longrightarrow 1$. L'H\^opital's
Rule also applies in the case of the
indeterminate form $\frac{\infty}{\infty}$.
\end{document}
```

This file can be called anything. Now just process the file normally with `pdflatex` to produce the final result.

If you don't have the `tikz` terminal available, you can almost definitely use the alternative method described in the next recipe, which introduces the `epslatex` terminal.

How it works...

The `tikz` terminal translates the plotting data into a list of drawing instructions in the TikZ language, which is a graphics language invented for use in LaTeX documents that is an interface to the lower-level PGF graphics language. It is installed in most modern LaTeX installations, and the `tikz` terminal is available starting with gnuplot version 4.4. (Nevertheless, some compilations of this version of gnuplot do not include this terminal, as it has some unusual dependencies.) You can draw "by hand" directly in the TikZ language; this can be a convenient way to create diagrams from within a LaTeX document. But for the charts and graphs that you might want to use gnuplot for, gnuplot can do this drawing for you.

The resulting file is a fragment of a LaTeX document consisting of the TikZ picture. It is meant to be included in your final document with the LaTeX `\input` command. Since the TikZ instructions are processed by LaTeX to produce the final picture, complicated graphs with many segments, such as large 3D plots, can take some time for LaTeX to chew through; far longer than gnuplot would take when creating such plots with one of the "normal" terminal drivers.

Since the text of labels, titles, and so on will be included directly in the LaTeX file, you can use almost any LaTeX construct in these strings (although, as mentioned in the previous recipe, the displayed math style needs to be invoked by using \displaystyle).

In your LaTeX document, you will need the line that is highlighted in the previous document fragment that loads the gnuplot-lua-tikz package. This package defines some commands that gnuplot uses in the TikZ picture. The lua part refers to a scripting language that gnuplot calls out to perform the processing that produces the TikZ instructions. Then simply \input the TikZ picture file where you would normally place an \includegraphics command for a normal picture, placing it inside a figure, floatingfigure, or other environment, if desired.

In order to scale the picture, you can use the \resizebox command as we did in the second highlighted line in the previous code snippet, but you can avoid this by making the picture the desired final size in gnuplot to begin with. Using the "!" in the arguments to \resizebox allows us to specify one of the dimensions, in this case the width, while retaining the figure's aspect ratio.

Remember that if you have used Unicode characters in any of your labels, you must include the inputenc package or some other package that allows LaTeX to deal with Unicode (fourth line in the previous example); but this has become standard practice lately, as it is very convenient to be able to use Unicode from within LaTeX.

Assembling a document using epslatex

If you have the tikz terminal available, you will most likely want to use it in situations such as those in the previous recipe, where you want to incorporate the results of the TeX typographical engine into your plots.

If tikz support happens not to be compiled into your version of gnuplot, you can achieve the same results using the older epslatex terminal. This is almost always available; you can check by typing set term and perusing the resulting long list of output devices that gnuplot knows about.

Using the tikz terminal for these purposes may lead to a simpler workflow, as it produces a TeX file that can be processed with pdflatex to produce a PDF file directly. This is what most people want to do most of the time, now that PDF has become the *de facto* standard for technical and scientific documents.

The epslatex terminal was designed for an earlier age when the only graphics format that could be included in LaTeX documents was encapsulated PostScript, and the final result of running TeX or LaTeX over your document was a DVI (device independent) file. Support for viewing these files is not widespread.

Fortunately, with one additional processing step, we can use the epslatex terminal to get exactly the same results, and in a PDF file too. In this recipe, we show how to generate the previous figure using a different method (there may be slight differences in spacing, as the generated figure may have a very slightly different size or margins).

How to do it...

The following steps are required to use the epslatex terminal:

Making the plot

Following is the gnuplot script for creating the graph:

```
set terminal epslatex
set out 'r4.tex'
unset key
set label '\Large$\displaystyle \lim_{x\Longrightarrow0}\frac{\sin(x)}
{x}=1$' at graph .55, .75
set title '\Large Illustrating Ls Rule: $\frac{\sin(x)}{x}$'
plot [0:15] sin(x)/x lw 2
```

The only change from the previous recipe is in the first line, where we have selected the epslatex terminal.

When this script is fed to gnuplot, it will create two files: a LaTeX document called r4.tex and an encapsulated PostScript file, containing the graph, called r4.eps.

The LaTeX document

Include the generated LaTeX file in your LaTeX document, as shown in the following listing:

```
\documentclass{article}
\usepackage{graphicx}
\usepackage[rflt]{floatflt}
\usepackage[T1]{fontenc}
\usepackage{textcomp}
\usepackage[utf8x]{inputenc}
\usepackage{gnuplot-lua-tikz}
\pagestyle{empty}
\begin{document}
\openup.5em
\begin{floatingfigure}{2.9in}
\resizebox{2.5in}{!}{\input{r4}}
\end{floatingfigure}
\noindent The figure to the right provides an illustration of L'H\^o\-
pi\-tal's Rule. Recall that this rule can be applied when taking the
limit as $x\longrightarrow x_a$ of a ratio of two functions where the
```

```
ratio approaches the indeterminate form $\frac{0}{0}$; in the case
where both functions are differentiable at $x_a$, the ratio approaches
the ratio of their derivatives. In the case illustrated both $\sin(x)$
and $x \longrightarrow0$ as we approach the origin, but the ratio of
their derivatives, $\frac{\cos(x)}{1} \longrightarrow 1$. L'H\^o\-pi\-
tal's Rule also applies in the case of the indeterminate form $\frac{\
infty}{\infty}$.
\end{document}
```

The only difference from the previous recipe is the name of the included file.

Producing the PDF

Assuming our final desired result is a PDF document, we must first transform the encapsulated PostScript file `r4.eps` into a PDF file. It doesn't matter how we do this, but one convenient method available on Linux is to use the command-line tool `epstopdf`, which does just what it says. On the Macintosh, if `epstopdf` is not installed, we need to merely open the EPS figure in Preview and then save it. Preview converts the file to PDF for display.

Once this is done, we need to simply run `pdflatex` on the file to get our final document.

Another workflow is to process our main document with the `latex` command, producing a DVI file. This can be converted, if desired, to a PDF file with the command-line tool `dvipdfm` or friends.

How it works...

When using the `epslatex` terminal, gnuplot will create two output files rather than the single file that we usually get. We will have our graph in the form of an encapsulated PostScript file with an `eps` extension. We will also have a LaTeX file with the name that we specify in the `set out` command. We should pick a filename with the extension `.tex` to make subsequent processing more convenient. The EPS file will have the same base name (name aside from the extension) as the one given in the `set out` command.

The LaTeX file generated by gnuplot need not normally be edited or looked at. Its job is to overlay all the text, including the tic and axis labels, title, and so on, onto the plot in the EPS file. If you look at the graph file itself (`r4.eps` in the example, or `r4.pdf` after conversion), you will see a bare plot with no labels or text.

Finally, our main document includes the LaTeX file created by gnuplot, which will in turn include the graph. We can include this file any way we wish, but usually we will put it in some sort of figure environment.

For most of the other details of how this recipe works, refer to the previous recipe.

Using gnuplot within LaTeX

In a previous recipe, we learned how to generate TikZ drawing commands from within gnuplot for inclusion in a LaTeX file. This recipe is, in a way, the reverse. We are going to learn how to generate gnuplot commands from within a LaTeX document.

The method introduced in this recipe is most useful when we want to enfold graphical elements into our typeset text rather than include them in floating figure environments. It also has the advantage of encompassing all the typesetting and drawing commands into a single file that is processed with one command, with no need to keep track of plot files and separate gnuplot scripts. This makes it simpler for your document source to become self-documenting and easily modifiable.

This is a flexible and powerful technique that allows us to combine plots generated by gnuplot with TikZ drawing commands. If we become proficient in TikZ, we will be able to arrange gnuplot graphs and PGF graphics in arbitrary ways on the page. As we don't have space here for a TikZ tutorial, we shall limit ourselves to the following simple example:

In the previous figure, we have a sentence typeset by LaTeX with some illustrations integrated into the line. The graphics were drawn by gnuplot and inserted back into the document by LaTeX, all automatically.

Getting ready

The technique we are going to learn now requires LaTeX, PGF, and gnuplot to work together to create a document with integrated text and graphics (PGF is the Portable Graphics Format, the actual drawing engine for which TikZ is a higher-level language). Unfortunately, there is an incompatibility between recent versions of gnuplot and all but the latest version of PGF. And, equally unfortunately, this latest version is not yet widely distributed. If, when trying this recipe, you see errors that complain about gnuplot not understanding "set term table" or something similar, then you need to upgrade your PGF installation. You can go to the official website at `http://pgf.sourceforge.net/` and download version 2.10, and follow the install instructions. After the files are copied to the correct places in the TeX tree, you will need to run `texhash` as root (or administrator).

How to do it...

The following single LaTeX file creates the illustration shown in the previous figure:

```
\documentclass{article}
\usepackage{tikz}
\usepackage{pgfplots}
\usepackage[T1]{fontenc}
\usepackage[utf8x]{inputenc}
\pagestyle{empty}
\begin{document}
A sinewave looks like \tikz\draw[domain=0:18.84, scale=.1] plot func
tion{sin(x)};
and a spiral looks like \tikz\draw[parametric, domain=0:18.84,
scale=.1]
    plot function{.2*t*cos(t),.2*t*sin(t)};.
\end{document}
```

This file must be processed with an extra argument to the `pdflatex` command that gives permission for the document to invoke an external program (in our case, gnuplot). This is for security; the concern is that malicious TeX documents might run programs without the user's knowledge, so you must turn on this ability manually. Usually, the command is `pdflatex --shell-escape file`, but on some systems it is `pdflatex --write18 file` (where, in both cases, you substitute the name of your TeX file for `file`, leaving off the `.tex` file extension).

How it works...

This will work in any LaTeX document, but we must be sure to include the `tikz` and `pgfplots` packages. The highlighted lines create the sentence shown in the previous illustration. When it's time to insert our pictures, we start the `\tikz` command, followed by `\draw` with the options in square brackets. The `domain` option serves the same purpose as the `[a:b] plot` notation within gnuplot; the `scale` option scales the final figure by the multiplicative factor supplied; and the `parametric` option means that the following plot command is a parametric function, with t as the parameter and the x and y coordinates separated by a comma (we covered parametric plotting in *Chapter 1, Plotting Curves, Boxes, Points, and more*).

A single command on our part is all that is required. LaTeX calls out to gnuplot automatically to create tables that are subsequently read in by PGF to create the illustrations, which are inserted into the page by the TeX typesetting engine. There will be a few auxiliary files left on the disc, which you can safely delete, but they may speed up subsequent passes through LaTeX if you are actively editing the file.

TikZ/PGF can produce any type of diagram, and TikZ pictures can be put inside of a floating figure environment, as we saw in the previous recipe. But where TikZ excels is the ease with which it can place small illustrations in line with the text. This can be done with the extensive graphical capabilities built into TikZ/PGF, which actually include the ability to make simple plots directly. As this is not a book about TikZ but about gnuplot, we've chosen to demonstrate how TikZ can use gnuplot as an external program. This is invoked with the **function** keyword in the highlighted line. If you want a full-blown graph with axes, tic marks, and so on, you can use other TikZ commands to create these, including LaTeX-typeset labels; but in this case you may be better off using the techniques of the previous two recipes.

Creating presentation slides with incrementally displayed graphs

Some explanation of the title of this recipe is in order. In ancient times, we gave presentations by putting sheets of plastic on "overhead projectors". We tended to put a great deal of information on each slide, as it was cumbersome to change them. Now that we plug computers into projectors and effortlessly flip back and forth through our slides, it is easier on the eyes to keep each slide relatively uncluttered and focused on a single idea.

One technique that aids this style of presentation is to create a kind of animation by having a series of slides where most of the content remains the same while one or two elements vary, focusing attention on the information conveyed by the changing elements. It gives the impression of an animation because the changing pieces can appear to move relative to the static content if the slides are changed quickly. This type of presentation is easy to create with gnuplot and the LaTeX **beamer** package, as shown in the following figure:

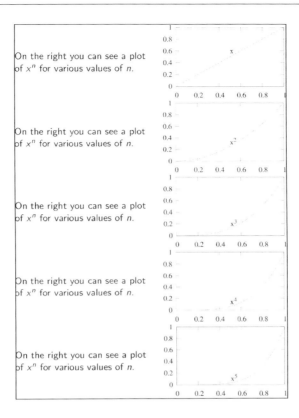

After running the code presented in the following *How to do it...* section you will have a five-page PDF file. If you set your PDF reader to display full-screen, or to display whole pages, and flip back and forth through the pages, you will see the effect that we are after.

The previous figure shows the five pages of the presentation with the page margins stripped out to save space.

Getting ready

As before, you will need a not-too-ancient installation of LaTeX. You will need the `beamer` package installed; this is included in most recent versions of the large LaTeX bundles, including TeXLive.

How to do it...

The following instructions will lead you to the presentation in the previous figure:

Making the plots

As was the case in several of the previous recipes in this chapter, we have two code samples. The first is our gnuplot script. After executing this with gnuplot, you should have five PDF pictures on your disc.

```
set term pdfcairo font "Times, 14" enhanced
unset key
set out 'p0.pdf'
set label 1 'x' at first .5, .5 + .1
plot [0:1] x
set out 'p1.pdf'
set label 1 'x^2' at first .5, .5**2 + .1
plot [0:1] x**2
set out 'p2.pdf'
set label 1 'x^3' at first .5, .5**3 + .1
plot [0:1] x**3
set out 'p3.pdf'
set label 1 'x^4' at first .5, .5**4 + .1
plot [0:1] x**4
set out 'p4.pdf'
set label 1 'x^5' at first .5, .5**4 + .1
plot [0:1] x**5
```

This script may appear to gnuplot experts to be unnecessarily verbose, but as we have not yet covered looping or other gnuplot programming constructs, we present the manual version. The next chapter will explain how to write scripts similar to the previous script with far fewer lines.

The LaTeX document

The following is the LaTeX file. Just run this once through `pdflatex` and in a couple of seconds you will have your final PDF presentation.

```
\documentclass{beamer}
\beamertemplatenavigationsymbolsempty
\usepackage[utf8]{inputenc}
\begin{document}
  \begin{frame}
    \begin{columns}[c,totalwidth=\textwidth]
    \column{.49\textwidth}
    On the right you can see a plot of $x^n$ for various values of
      $n$.
    \column{.51\textwidth}
```

```
        \includegraphics<1>[width=\textwidth]{p0.pdf}
        \includegraphics<2>[width=\textwidth]{p1.pdf}
        \includegraphics<3>[width=\textwidth]{p2.pdf}
        \includegraphics<4>[width=\textwidth]{p3.pdf}
        \includegraphics<5>[width=\textwidth]{p4.pdf}
      \end{columns}
    \end{frame}
  \end{document}
```

How it works...

We'll explain the gnuplot script and the LaTeX document in the following sections:

The gnuplot script

There should be nothing unfamiliar in the gnuplot script. We've chosen the `pdfcairo` terminal because we want a vector graphics format: when projected on a large screen, bitmapped graphics are likely to reveal their pixellated nature. The font specification is really necessary, as the default is too small to be legible from the back rows. We also want enhanced text, so we can use a superscript when labeling the curves. After turning off the legend, we have a repeated set of three commands; each set opens a new output file, redefines a label that is tagged with the number 1, and draws the plot. The label commands use the `first` coordinate system, so we can easily make the labels stick with their curves as the curves change.

The LaTeX document

The LaTeX script is merely a skeleton, containing a minimal working example to illustrate the technique, and obviously not a complete presentation. In a real presentation, you will have a title, authors, and other information that will appear on each slide, and we hope the content would be more interesting. The `beamer` class is one of several available classes for making presentations with LaTeX; I have tried several and feel that this is the best one. By default, beamer places navigation widgets on each slide, which we can turn off with the second line in the example document. The presentation is divided into **frames**, which may in turn be divided into subframes using the angle bracket notation. The command `\includegraphics<1>[width=\textwidth]{p0.pdf}`, for example, means that the file `p0.pdf` is to be included only in subframe 1 of the current frame. The `textwidth` here actually refers to the width of the column, which is 0.51 times the textwidth of the entire frame.

Since gnuplot is exceptionally good for automating the creation of sequences of plots, either using its built-in scripting language or other programming languages (as we are soon to see in the next chapter), its combination with the LaTeX beamer package forms a powerful system for creating the highest quality technical presentations. Since PDF is an open format for which free readers exist on every platform, this is also an excellent way to create educational material that can be distributed through the Web as well as projected for an audience.

Including a plot in a web page

Gnuplot can produce graphs in several formats that can be included in web pages. The chief purpose of this recipe is to give complete examples of current best practices for assembling web pages with graphics. Following is a screenshot from the display area of a web browser:

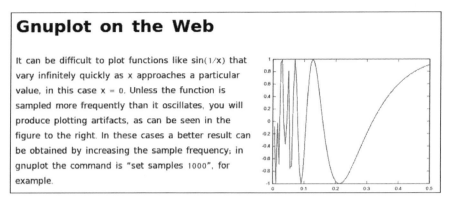

The text and figure are the same as in the previous recipe, *Adding a plot to a paper using LaTeX*.

How to do it...

The following sections will help you in including a plot in a web page as shown in the previous figure:

The gnuplot script

We'll modify our previous gnuplot script a little to produce an SVG file rather than a PDF file:

```
set term svg font "Arial,12"
set out 'r6fig.svg'
unset key
plot [0:.5] sin(1/x) lw 2
```

The HTML source

Following is a minimal HTML5 web page, showing the first method for including an SVG image:

```
<!DOCTYPE HTML>
<html>
  <head>
  <meta content="text/html;charset=utf-8" http-equiv="Content-Type"
    />
  <title>Gnuplot on the Web</title></head>
```

```
<body>
  <h1>Gnuplot on the Web</h1>
  <img src = "r6fig.svg" style = "float:right;" width = "300" alt =
  ""/>
  <p>
    It can be difficult to plot functions like sin(1/x) that vary
    infinitely quickly as x approaches a particular value, in this
    case x = 0. Unless the function is sampled more frequently than
    it oscillates, you will produce plotting artifacts, as can be
    seen in the figure to the right. In these cases a better result
    can be obtained by increasing the sample frequency;in gnuplot
    the command is  "set samples 1000", for example.
  </p>
</body>
</html>
```

After making sure that the file r6fig.svg is in the same directory as the HTML file, open the file in any modern, graphical web browser; you should see a page displayed similar to the previous figure (the typeface and some other details may be different depending on the preferences set in your browser).

How it works...

The first line in the HTML code sample tells the browser that this is an HTML5 document. This is the current standard for web pages and is supported in all modern browsers; since it is backward compatible, there is no reason not to use it. Nevertheless, the example should work for older HTML standards as well, with their more verbose DOCTYPEs.

The img tag selects the SVG file that we created with our gnuplot script in the src attribute; the float:right style does the same thing as the floatingfigure environment in the previous LaTeX recipe.

 SVG is the only vector graphics format that can be viewed on the Web without a plugin.

Other choices for image formats that we might have used include PNG and JPEG; but as SVG files are now well supported in all recent browser versions, we want to use this high quality vector format whenever possible. If you are compelled to use one of the bitmapped formats in your web page, the HTML syntax for their inclusion is precisely the same as in the example code.

There's more...

You can open the SVG file in an editor and change it, or write one by hand: the format is XML text. You can also include this file (more precisely, the parts between the SVG tags, excluding the header lines before the opening tag) directly within your HTML page, rather than by reference. This allows you to do other things, such as make the image interactive and modify it with JavaScript. However, support for inline SVG is still not quite as widespread as support for including SVG images by reference in `img` tags or others. Also, there is another problem. I have discovered that the SVG files created by gnuplot, although they seem to work, are not strictly valid. The reader can verify this by using the validator at `http://validator.w3.org/`. This means that if they are included directly in your HTML pages, they will render your pages invalid as well.

Making an interactive plot for the Web [new]

gnuplot's new **canvas** terminal allows us to include a graph in a web page with some interactive widgets:

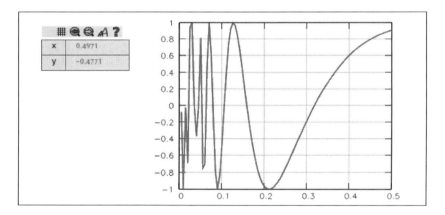

Getting ready

As before, in order to see the results of this recipe, you will need a decently modern graphical web browser, in this case with JavaScript enabled (which it will most likely be by default, if you have not disabled it or installed a script-blocking extension). This recipe depends on gnuplot at least at version 4.4; the canvas terminal that we'll be using in this recipe is a new feature in gnuplot.

The HTML file created by the use of this recipe will refer to three JavaScript files and one CSS (Cascading Style Sheet) file that were installed on your machine when gnuplot was installed. These are called `gnuplot_common.js`, `gnuplot_mouse.js`, `canvastext.js`, and `gnuplot_mouse.css`. Usually, especially on a Unix-type operating system, you will find these files in `/usr/local/share/gnuplot/4.4/js`. It is probably most convenient for you to copy these files now into the directory where you will be running the scripts and developing your page; but for deployment, you will need to copy these to a public URL and point to their location using an option to the `canvas` terminal (explained in the following *There's more...* section).

How to do it...

Run the following script through gnuplot:

```
set term canvas size 400,300 standalone mousing
set out 'Making_an_interactive_plot_for_the_web.html'
unset key
set grid
plot [0:.5] sin(1/x) lw 2
```

You will find a new file on your disc with the title given in the `set out` command. If you view this HTML file in a web browser that supports the `canvas` element, you will see a familiar plot along with some mouseable widgets. The previous figure shows how this page should appear, but you will have to run the script and open the page in your browser to see the interactive plot in operation. You can toggle the grid on and off, zoom with the middle (right in some browsers) mouse button, and flip back and forth through the zoom levels, just as you can do in the X11 or wxt interactive terminals when using gnuplot on your computer. There is also a table that displays the x and y coordinates or your pointer position as you move the mouse pointer around the graph.

How it works...

The highlighted line selects the `canvas` terminal, which, in **standalone** mode, assembles a web page (with a missing DOCTYPE) containing a canvas element and an embedded JavaScript program that draws the graph into the canvas, as well as constructs the interactive widgets and connects them to functions that perform zooming and toggling the grid. This is a convenient starting point to which you can add the rest of your web page text, which would probably include something explaining what the graph is about.

There's more...

If you examine the generated HTML file, you will see references to the JavaScript libraries where they live in your gnuplot installation. This is fine for use on your own computer, but if you want to deploy these pages on the public Web, you will need to make these libraries accessible. We can do this by passing the `jsdir` parameter to the `set term canvas` command, for example, `set term canvas jsdir 'http://example.com/gnuplot/javascript/' size . . . .` This will change these file references to point to this directory, where presumably we have put the `gnuplot_common.js` files.

The ability of gnuplot to create interactive graphs in web pages continues to develop in recent builds that have not yet been released as official gnuplot versions. One exciting capability that appeared recently allows the creation of interactive SVG plots, where different plot elements can be toggled on and off with the mouse, while retaining all the transparency and other capabilities of the SVG terminal. If you are interested in creating interactive plots for the Web, then you should follow gnuplot development progress closely.

[The Appendix lists sources of information about gnuplot and its ongoing development.]

7
Programming gnuplot and Dealing with Data

This chapter contains the following recipes:

- ▶ Scripting gnuplot with its own language
- ▶ Plotting on subintervals
- ▶ Smoothing your data
- ▶ Fitting functions to your data
- ▶ Using kdensity smoothing to improve on histograms [new]
- ▶ Creating a cumulative distribution [new]
- ▶ Talking to gnuplot with C
- ▶ Scripting gnuplot with Python
- ▶ Plotting with Clojure
- ▶ Handling volatile data [new]

Introduction

Up to now our style of interacting with gnuplot has mainly been to have an interactive conversation at the terminal, or to create a linear sequence of commands that can be read in and executed by typing `gnuplot file`. We went beyond this a bit in the previous chapter, where we learned how to arrange for a document preparation system to invoke gnuplot automatically. In this chapter, we shall learn how to leverage the full power of gnuplot as a programmable graphing engine. This is made possible by gnuplot's design as a program that can be completely controlled by textual commands, rather than by a limited graphical user interface. This means that any programming language that can send text to a process or socket can send commands to gnuplot. The result is that there are libraries for interfacing with gnuplot in almost every high-level programming or scripting language, and even in cases where no library is available it is straightforward to communicate manually from within your program, as we shall see. In addition, gnuplot's own built-in scripting language contains enough programming constructs to allow significant automation without the use of another language.

Another set of topics we visit in this chapter are gnuplot's built-in smoothing algorithms, including two immensely useful types of statistical plots that are new in version 4.4. We end the chapter with a recipe introducing gnuplot's new ability to deal gracefully with data that may be changing under your feet as you try to work with it.

Scripting gnuplot with its own language

We have learned how to use a large number of gnuplot commands and assembled them into scripts, included with this book as code samples, that can be executed from the command line or read in from the gnuplot's interactive plot with the `load` command. Up to now, however, these scripts have taken the form of a simple sequence of commands, each one to be executed once; the same result is obtained whether we enter the commands one at a time at the prompt or load the script as a whole, in batch mode.

There are many tasks that are much more convenient, and others that are only possible, if we can apply some sort of automation to the generation of commands. Fortunately, gnuplot, as part of its command language, includes a simple facility for applying some basic programming constructs. There is a basic looping control, a way to iterate over a set of commands, and an `if—then—else` statement. With these few borrowings from procedural languages, we can do a great deal; and, as we shall see later on in the chapter, if we need more, we can control gnuplot from within almost any general-purpose programming language. In the following figure, the Bessel function is plotted five times, each time with its argument scaled differently, with a different linetype for each curve, and with a curve title for the legend constructed individually for each plot:

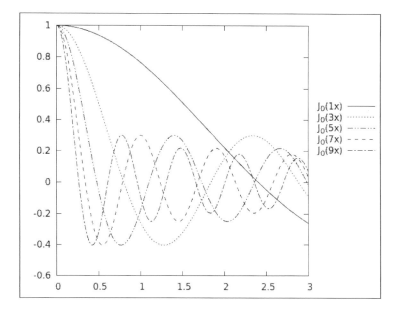

How to do it...

The previous graph could have been made by issuing five individual plot commands, but in fact was produced with a single line highlighted in the following gnuplot script:

```
set term pngcairo mono dashed enhanced
set out "file.png"
set rmargin at screen .8
set key at screen 1,.7
plot [0 : 3] for [n = 1 : 10 : 2] besj0(n*x) title "J_0(".n."x)" lt n
```

How it works...

The selection of terminal type and output file in the first two lines may be familiar from previous chapters. This recipe will work for any terminal type, so these details are not crucial; however, we want to select `enhanced` text handling so we can use subscripts in the legend, and we've also specified dashed monochrome plot curves so the different lines can be distinguished in black and white output, as in the printed version of this book.

The highlighted line contains the new concept for this recipe: within the `plot` command is embedded a new construct. The `for` keyword introduces a loop iteration similar to the *for* loop in C and similar languages. The loop variable (in this case n) is introduced within the square brackets; the notation here means that n goes from 1 to 10 in steps of 2: 1, 3, 5, 7, 9. The plot command is repeated for each value of n, and wherever n appears in the command its value is substituted. The result is that this one compact line, highlighted in the script, is equivalent to the long, compound plot command:

```
plot [0 : 3] besj0(1*x) title "J_0(1x)" lt 1, \
             besj0(2*x) title "J_0(2x)" lt 2, \
...
```

When constructing our curve titles, we've used the **string catenation** operator, which is a dot; when integers are joined with strings in gnuplot, the integers (the variable n here) are first **typecast** to strings.

We have enlarged the right margin with the `set rmargin` command, and specified a location for the legend with the `set key` command, using screen coordinates, to place the key outside the plot on the right. This is helpful when there are many curves in a plot that might collide with the legend.

There's more...

The `for` loop is available in the plot command, as demonstrated in the previous script, and also in the `set` command, where it can be used, for example, to define a whole series of user `linestyles` (see *Chapter 3, Applying Colors and Styles*) all at once.

But gnuplot has a more flexible style of iteration that we can turn to when its simple `for` loop is not sufficient. This is accomplished with the use of the `reread` keyword in conjunction with an `if` statement, as shown in the following script:

```
plot sin(0.1*n*x)
n = n + 1
if (n < 100) reread
```

In order to use this code block, we must first save it in a file (the code has been included as a supplemental sample for this recipe). Start up gnuplot and get the interactive prompt. Then set the variable n to 1 by simply saying n = 1. If we wish, we can now set terminal and other options; let's set the terminal to one of the onscreen terminals such as X11 or wxt, and say `set samples 1000` for a smooth plot. Now, if we say `load file`, substituting the name of the file where we saved the previous code sample, we should see a nice animation of a sine wave sweeping from a low to a high frequency.

This happens because of the final (highlighted) line. The last word on that line, `reread`, is a special keyword that tells gnuplot to go back to the beginning of the file and execute it again. But each time the file is loaded, the value of n is incremented by the second line, and it is retained. This could continue forever, but is terminated by the `if` clause, which only executes the `reread` when n is less than 100. Instead of displaying an animation on the screen, we could have saved each plot to a separate file by incorporating the n variable into a filename using the string catenation operator (set out "file".n."png" would do it). Then, we could use any of a number of programs to stitch the files together into a movie. In this way, gnuplot's simple iteration facilities can be used to create animations for presentations or teaching. The recipe *Creating presentation slides with incrementally displayed graphs* in *Chapter 6, Including Plots in Documents* contained a script that produced a series of graphs for inclusion into a presentation. Using the looping technique introduced in this recipe, we can now see how this script could be written more concisely, and with less chance for typos to creep in.

Plotting on subintervals

gnuplot has built-in a respectable collection of special functions and mathematical operators that allow us to perform significant calculations and massaging of data before plotting. A complete survey of gnuplot's math brain is beyond the scope of this book; interested readers should start with *Chapter 13* of the official reference manual distributed with the program and available at http://gnuplot.info/documentation.html.

Here, we shall merely give an example of one very useful technique for plotting functions that have different definitions over different domains; this technique works equally well for functions that are continuous or discontinuous over the entire plotting domain. The example will demonstrate several of gnuplot's mathematical facilities that have not been covered up to now. Following figure is a plot of two functions, a simple sine wave that turns into a decaying sine wave when we cross x = 0:

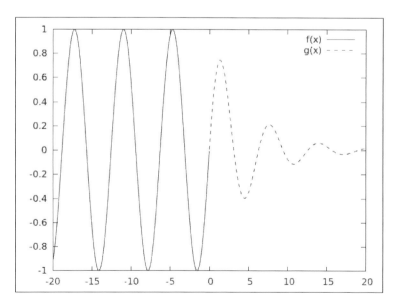

How to do it...

The following script will produce the previous plot:

```
set samples 2000
f(x) = x < 0 ? sin(x) : NaN
g(x) = x >= 0 ? exp(-x/5.)*sin(x) : NaN
plot [-20 : 20] f(x), g(x)
```

How it works...

The highlighted lines contain the new features for this recipe. gnuplot allows us to define our own functions, which can save typing later. The first highlighted line defines a function f(x). Its definition employs the ternary operator, which works in gnuplot similar to the way it works in C and some other programming languages. The structure is C ? A : B, where C is a condition, in this case that x is less than 0. If the condition is true, then A is read and the rest of the structure is skipped; if B is true, then C is read and A is ignored. In the example, f(x) is defined to be sin(x) for negative x and **NaN** otherwise. NaN stands for Not A Number. gnuplot will not plot anything for NaN, so this is a way to make part of a graph blank; this does what we want, since f(x) is undefined for positive or zero x and we don't want anything plotted there. (Another way to construct an undefined value that will cause gnuplot to not plot anything is to use 1/0 instead of NaN.)

By now it should be clear what the second highlighted line does. It creates a function g(x), which is only defined for nonnegative x, where it is defined as an expression that may be taken to represent a frictionally damped oscillator.

The final line is a familiar plot command that refers to our two user-defined functions. Notice that we have set the number of samples to a fairly large number. This is to avoid having a gap between the two different functions, which do in fact have the same value at x = 0.

Note on division:

Although we said that we're not going to give a complete course on math in gnuplot, we would like to mention one issue that tends to trip up newcomers, and even some experienced users. In the gnuplot interactive prompt, type print 1/2 and print 5/2. If the results are what you expected, read no farther. If you are surprised, here's what's going on. In the expressions you typed, the numbers were integers, since they had no decimal points. In common with many programming languages, gnuplot returns an integer result when you ask it to do a mathematical operation on integers—and the way it casts a number to an integer is to discard the noninteger component, which has the effect of rounding down. If you want a floating-point result, you need to write at least one of the numbers with a decimal point. For example, 1.0/2 will yield 0.5.

Smoothing your data

As an option to the `plot` command, gnuplot offers several smoothing functions. The name *smooth* is a bit misleading. Included in the options for the `smooth` plotstyle are several ways to process your data that would not most naturally be described as *smoothing*. We give examples of some of these in the following recipes. In the current recipe we show how to use the smoothing option that seems to be most immediately useful if you have some noisy data and want to draw a qualitatively smooth curve through it, to, as they say, guide the eye.

Getting ready

This recipe uses the datafile `rs.dat`; make sure that it is in your current directory. This file contains two columns that are the *x* and *y* coordinates of a simple sine wave of frequency and amplitude 1 to which normally distributed random data centered on 0 is added; that is, a sine curve plus the type of noise that might arise from actual measurements. In the following figure, we have a plot of the noisy sine wave, plotted with a thin line, overlaid with a thick curve showing the **bezier smoothed** approximation to the data, computed by gnuplot:

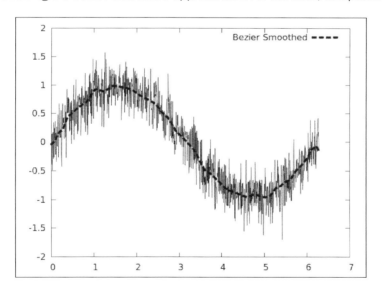

How to do it...

Use the following script to obtain the previous figure:

```
plot 'rs.dat' with lines lw 0.5 notitle, \
     '' smooth bezier lw 4 title "Bezier Smoothed"
```

How it works...

The `plot` command is broken over two lines to make it easier to read; we've used one of gnuplot's *special filenames*, namely the empty string, which stands for the datafile previously read in, to avoid typing its name twice. The first part of the plot command is straightforward; we've asked for a thin line so that the smoothed overlay will be easier to see, and decided that we don't want a name for this curve to appear in the legend. The second part of the plot command contains the new feature `smooth bezier`; this tells gnuplot to compute a bezier curve to fit the data and plot that rather than the data itself. We see that the smoothed curve does a nice job of graphically summarizing the trend in the data, although it is a little bumpy. This is considered a simple smoothing option, and there are no adjustments for it.

Fitting functions to your data

If we want to get serious about fitting functions to our data, we can turn to gnuplot's sophisticated **fit** command.

Getting ready

You need the same datafile used in the previous recipe, `rs.dat`. The following figure shows the same noisy sine wave, but this time the overlaid curve seems to be perfectly smooth:

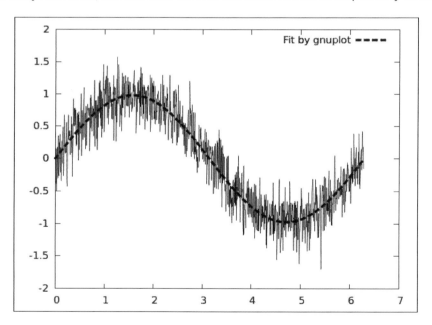

How to do it...

The following script will produce the previous figure:

```
f(x) = a*sin(b*x)
fit f(x) 'rs.dat' via a, b
plot 'rs.dat' with lines lw 0.5 notitle, f(x) lw 4 title "Fit by
gnuplot"
```

How it works...

gnuplot's `fit` command takes a function defined by the user containing several parameters and attempts to find the set of values for these parameters that result in the best fit of the resulting function to the data specified. *Best fit* is in a nonlinear least-squares sense that is thoroughly discussed in the official gnuplot manual. After entering the `fit` command, gnuplot will iterate, displaying intermediate results on the console, until it finds an acceptable fit. At that point, the parameters have been assigned the optimum values and, if desired, the fitting function can be plotted, as we did in this recipe.

First, we define `f(x)` to be our fitting function. We can choose any function or expression that returns a floating-point value; our choice is informed by the fact that we happen to know that our data is based on a sine wave. We are pretending that we don't know its frequency or amplitude, letting these be represented by the fitting parameters b and a.

The second (highlighted) line tells gnuplot to calculate the `fit` by varying the parameters following the keyword `via`. After it's done, these parameters hold the resulting values. In the last line, we plot the original data and our fitting function. We see that gnuplot calculated the frequency and amplitude correctly, which is apparent from the plot and from the output on the console.

Using kdensity smoothing to improve on histograms [new]

In *Chapter 1, Plotting Curves, Boxes, Points, and more*, we saw how to plot histograms, which are a type of statistical plot that show how a set of data is distributed: how many samples lie within each range of values, or *bin*. There are problems with histograms, venerable as they are, however. For example, the apparent shape of the distribution depends in part on how big we make our bins. Histogram plots can be misleading, and do not always serve the statistical purpose for which they were intended.

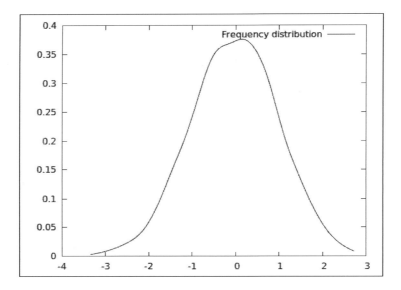

For these reasons and others, statisticians have invented other ways to calculate and display information about the distribution of a collection of data. One of these is called the **kernel density estimate**, which may be thought of as a kind of smoothed, bin-independent histogram. This is built into gnuplot as a plotting style—an option to the smooth style. This is a new feature in gnuplot version 4.4.

Getting ready

Make sure you are in a directory with the supplied datafile called randomnormal.text. This is a single column of numbers generated with a random number generator that claims to produce random data with a normal (Gaussian, or bell curve) distribution. Parameters were chosen so that the underlying distribution is supposed to be centered on 0 and have a standard deviation of 1.

How to do it...

The previous figure is the output of the following script:

```
plot 'randomnormal.text' using 1:(.001) smooth kdensity \
     title "Frequency distribution
```

How it works...

The highlighted words in the previous script choose the smoothing option that calculates the kernel density estimate. This calculation uses the second column to weight the individual data points. Since we want each point to have equal weight, we substitute an expression equal to the reciprocal of the number of data points; this will lead to a normalized distribution curve, where the area under the curve should be equal to 1, and the area between two x values equals the probability of getting a random number that lies between those two values.

We see in the previous figure that the distribution appears to be approximately Gaussian in shape and that its maximum and standard deviation seem to be about right, so our random number generator is working as advertised.

Creating a cumulative distribution [new]

In this recipe, we show how to use another useful statistical plot hiding away in the smoothing options, and also new to gnuplot in version 4.4. The curve plotted in the next figure is closely related to the one plotted in the previous recipe. To get the following figure, just integrate the frequency distribution curve:

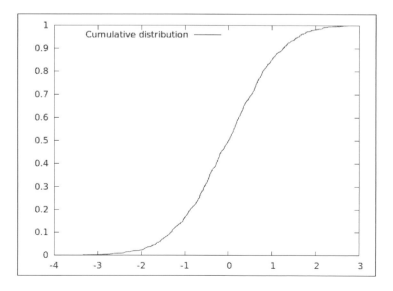

Getting ready

Make sure you are in a directory with the supplied datafile called `randomnormal.text`.

How to do it...

The following script will get you the previous figure:

```
set key top left
plot 'randomnormal.text' using 1:(.001) smooth cumul \
     title "Cumulative distribution"
```

How it works...

The normalization issues are the same as the kdensity discussion in the previous recipe. The only difference here is the choice of `smooth cumul`—an abbreviation for `cumulative`. We can verify that we have a properly normalized curve because it approaches **1** as we approach the endpoint on the right. This is what we should expect, because this curve gives the integral, or area, under the normalized distribution curve plotted in the previous recipe. This cumulative distribution curve tells us the probability of choosing, for any x value, a random number equal to or less than x.

Talking to gnuplot with C

In this and the next few recipes, we are going to demonstrate how to use gnuplot from within different programming languages. There are no illustrations for these recipes, as we are not giving examples of particular types of plots. We provide samples of code for several languages that you can modify to get started immediately incorporating gnuplot's plotting facilities into your programs.

The first example was chosen to demonstrate that we can use gnuplot from within almost any programming language, even if no specialized library exists for that purpose.

Getting ready

You need to have a C compiler installed to follow along here. Just about any Unix-type operating system, including Linux and Macintosh (if the Developer Tools have been installed) comes with one, and it is usually called `gcc`.

How to do it...

Compile the following program with `gcc file.c`, where `file.c` is the name of the file in which it is saved (the example distributed with this book that is named after this recipe is `Talking_to_gnuplot_with_C.c`):

```c
#include <stdio.h>
void main()
{
    FILE* gnuplot;
    gnuplot = popen("gnuplot -persist", "w");
    if (gnuplot != NULL)
    fprintf(gnuplot, "plot sin(1/x)\n");
}
```

You should now have a file called `a.out`, which you can execute by typing `./a.out`. The plot should appear instantly. (These instructions will work for Linux, Macintosh, or any normal Unix-derived operating system.)

How it works...

The key to this technique is the `popen` function, which allows us to talk to a process as if it we were writing to a file. The gnuplot process is started with `-persist` so that when the program is run, the plot stays up on the screen; otherwise it would vanish as soon as the program exits. After opening the pipe to gnuplot, we can send a series of commands just as if we were sitting at the interactive prompt, using print statements. The code sample is a minimal working skeleton of code to demonstrate the technique; in a real program you can read data, perform any desired calculations, and save plots to files. And this technique will work in almost any programming language that contains facilities for starting external processes and sending strings to them.

Scripting gnuplot with Python

In this recipe, we turn to the scripting language Python. This high-level language is well suited to the interactive exploration of data and the rapid development of programs for its analysis. This facility is made even stronger by its extension library `numpy`, which adds a rich set of efficient, C-coded routines for manipulating numerical arrays. In addition, there are several ways to make plots directly from Python. In this recipe we introduce Python's gnuplot interface, `gnuplot.py`.

Getting ready

You will need an installation of Python and its numerical library `numpy`, which comes with several popular scientific Python packages. You also need `gnuplot.py`, which you also may already have if you are doing scientific work with Python. If not, you can download it from its official Sourceforge site at `http://gnuplot-py.sourceforge.net/`.

How to do it...

Run the following code by typing **python file.py**, substituting the name of the Python script for `file` (the included sample is called `Scripting_gnuplot_with_Python.py`):

```
from numpy import *
import Gnuplot
g = Gnuplot.Gnuplot()
g.title('My Favorite Plot')
g.xlabel('x')
g.ylabel('sin(1/x)')
g('set term pngcairo')
g('set out "GnuplotFromPython.png"')
g('plot sin(1/x)')
```

You should then have a PNG file with your plot in your current directory.

How it works...

After importing the Gnuplot package and setting a variable equal to the function `Gnuplot.Gnuplot()`, we can issue commands directly to gnuplot just by passing strings to `g`. The details of starting the process and opening the pipe, that we did manually in the previous recipe, are taken care of for us automatically by the `gnuplot.py` package. The package also contains many abstracted gnuplot commands, such as the `g.title()` function shown in the example. Read the demo files and documentation that come with the `gnuplot.py` download to find out everything else it can do.

There's more...

The previous example is a bit contrived; if all you could do with the Python-gnuplot interface was to send commands that you could just as easily issue directly from the gnuplot interactive prompt, it would be of limited utility. The real value of this package is its ability to plot arrays calculated from within our Python program. The following program is included as the file `Scripting_gnuplot_with_Python_2.py`:

```
from numpy import *
import Gnuplot
g = Gnuplot.Gnuplot()
```

```
g.title('Normally Distributed Random Data')
g.xlabel('x')
g.ylabel('y')
g('set term pngcairo')
g('set out "GnuplotFromPython2.png"')
x = arange(1, 1000)
y = [random.normal() for i in x]
g.plot(Gnuplot.Data(x, y))
```

In the last line, we've used another abstraction provided by the `gnuplot.py` package, `Gnuplot.Gnuplot().plot()`, combined with the `Gnuplot.Data()` object, to plot one python `numpy` array (or list cast to an array) versus another. In fact, the array stored in `y` uses the random number generator that we probed in the previous recipes introducing the `smooth kdensity` and `smooth cumulative` plot commands.

Plotting with Clojure

Clojure is a dialect of lisp that is implemented on the Java Virtual Machine, so it is easy to install and run almost anywhere. The details can be found at `http://clojure.org/`. As this book is being prepared Clojure is rapidly becoming popular, as it is gaining recognition as perhaps the most practical implementation of an early high-level language that many consider to be the most powerful ever devised. Although Clojure is still in a somewhat early stage of adoption, it is quite mature, used in large projects and by big companies, and you can use gnuplot from it.

Getting ready

You need, naturally, an installation of the Clojure language. You may be able to install it using your package manager if you are using a Linux distribution (it is available in Ubuntu, for example); otherwise, you can download it from its official page at `http://clojure.org/downloads`. We are using the program **clojure-gnuplot** by Vadim Shender, so you should get that from `https://bitbucket.org/vshender/clojure-gnuplot`. After unzipping the `clojure-gnuplot` download, copy the directory tree `org/shender`, which is under `src` and contains the single file `clojure_gnuplot.clj`, to the place on your machine where you keep your Java classfiles and where you will likely find `clojure.jar` itself. On Linux this is typically `/usr/share/java`. Now, you can start Clojure by typing `CLASSPATH=/usr/share/java clojure` and the `require` statement in the first line of the script will work.

How to do it...

Execute the following code in the Clojure REPL (the interactive prompt, also known as the 'Reval-Eval-Print-Loop'):

```
(require '[org.shender.clojure-gnuplot :as gnuplot])
(def gp (gnuplot/start))
```

```
(gnuplot/exec gp
 (unset key)
 (set xrange (range -5 5))
 (plot (sin (/ 1 x)) with dots))
(gnuplot/stop gp)
```

If you execute all but the last line of this code sample in the Clojure REPL, you will see your plot on the screen. The final line stops the gnuplot process and destroys the plot.

How it works...

The first line imports the symbols from `clojure-gnuplot`. This interface code, which fits on half a page, defines a macro and several functions that rearrange the Clojure syntax into the conventional infix syntax understood by gnuplot. The result is that you can enter gnuplot commands in your program using a lispy syntax.

Handling volatile data [new]

Older versions of gnuplot ran into a problem when dealing, for example, with datafiles whose content is subject to change. When using gnuplot to examine such **volatile** data interactively, we might want to zoom in or out, or add a title to the plot to prepare it for saving. The problem is that each of these operations either requires an explicit call to `replot` or, in the case of mouse operations, calls it implicitly. And when the `replot` command is issued, the datafile is read anew, and the new data is plotted. What if we want to manipulate the plot while retaining the data already read in?

The new features in gnuplot version 4.4 for dealing with volatile data were added with these issues in mind.

How to do it...

The volatile data source

In order to play with this feature, it is convenient to have some volatile data available. If you run the following Python program, supplied as the code sample `randomnormalIntervals.py`, in the background, it will make a datafile and replace it with new data every three seconds. This is the normally distributed random number data familiar from previous recipes. Don't forget to kill the program when you are finished, because otherwise it will run forever. The following is a listing of the program for producing the volatile data stream:

```
from numpy import *
import time
def makeit():
  f = open('randomnormal.text', 'w')
```

```
   a = [f.write("%g\n" % (random.normal())) for v in range(0, 1000)]
   f.close()
while True:
  makeit()
  time.sleep(3)
```

On most Unix-type systems, you can just type **python randomnormalIntervals.py &** to run the program in the background.

Handling the data with gnuplot

Now start gnuplot and type the following command:

```
plot 'randomnormal.text' volatile
```

The `volatile` keyword tells gnuplot that the file contains data that might change, and the values read in should be retained until a `replot` is issued.

Now try zooming in and out, and adding some features to the plot:

```
set title "Volatile Data"
```

When you want to see your changes, type:

```
refresh
```

Note that your title and other things are added, but the actual plot has not changed; although by now the data on disc is different, the previously read data is still being used. You are in control, and can see the new data when you want with the following command:

```
replot
```

Now you see a plot of fresh data along with any changes to the plotting parameters that you've specified.

Now type the following command without the `volatile` keyword:

```
plot 'randomnormal.text'
```

You will see that every time you use the mouse to zoom in or out, new data is read in and plotted; you cannot manipulate the plot while retaining previously read data.

How it works...

The new command `refresh` is activated when you tell gnuplot that it is plotting `volatile` data. This command will replot using the previously read-in data, which is retained in memory, rather than the data as it currently exists. The interactive zooming and mouse controls will implicitly issue a `refresh` rather than a `replot` when the data is marked as `volatile`. To read in the current data and plot it, use the `replot` command. gnuplot will automatically treat piped-in or inline data as volatile.

8

The Third Dimension

This chapter contains the following recipes:

- ▶ Making a surface plot
- ▶ Using coordinate mappings
- ▶ Coloring the surface
- ▶ Making a contour plot
- ▶ Making a vector plot
- ▶ Making an image plot or heat map
- ▶ Combining contours and images
- ▶ Combining surfaces with images
- ▶ Plotting a path in 3D
- ▶ Drawing parametric surfaces

Introduction

Every graph we have seen so far in this book has been a plot of one quantity versus another quantity, or in the case of parametric plots, two coordinates that depend on a single third parameter. These are called two dimensional (2D) plots. In this chapter, we break into the third dimension. The graphs here are visualizations of quantities that depend on two variables; they are expressed as surfaces, contours, fields of arrows, paths in space, or as a combination of these elements.

Making a surface plot

A surface plot represents the dependent quantity z, which depends on the two independent variables x and y, as a surface whose height indicates the value of z.

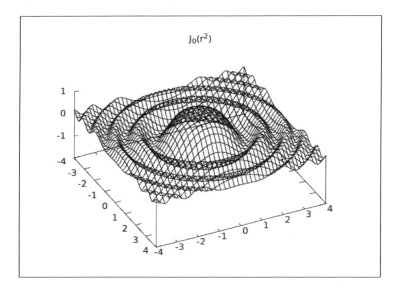

The previous figure is a perspective drawing of a surface representing the Bessel function $J0(r)$, where r is the distance from (x=0, y=0). The height of the surface shows the value of J0, given on the vertical axis (unlabeled in this figure, but usually called z). The other two (unlabeled) axes defining the plane above which the surface is drawn are the x and y axes.

How to do it...

The following code listing is the script that coaxed gnuplot into making the previous figure:

```
set isosamples 40
unset key
set title "J_0(r^2)"
set xrange [-4:4]
set yrange [-4:4]
set ztics 1
splot besj0(x**2+y**2)
set view 29,53 #Done implicitly by mousing.
set term pngcairo mono enhanced
set out 'bessel.png'
replot
```

How it works...

There are several new commands in this recipe. The `set isosamples` command sets the **isoline density**. This is analogous to the `set samples` command when making 2D plots, but it sets the number of lines used in forming the surface. The number of isosamples can be set independently in each direction; if one number is specified, it is used for both directions. The default of 10 usually creates surfaces that are far too coarse to be useful.

Turning to the second of the highlighted commands, the `splot` command is the 3D version of our old friend the `plot` command (it probably initially stood for "surface plot", but now can do several things besides plot surfaces, as we shall see in the rest of this chapter). It expects a function of x and y rather than x alone. Although we are interested in plotting something that has the type of symmetry that would be most conveniently expressed in polar (spherical or cylindrical) coordinates, these geometries are not available for function plots in 3D in gnuplot. (They are available through the `set mapping` command for data plots, as we shall see later in this chapter.) Therefore in such cases, we are required to convert our expressions to the rectangular coordinate system. Instead of what we would call `r` in a cylindrical coordinate system, here we use the equivalent `x**2 + y**2`.

In this recipe, we would like to illustrate, as far as possible, the interactive approach to creating a final 3D plot. The next highlighted line, beginning with `set view`, can be entered on the command line or included in a script. The `view` is the orientation in degrees of the perspective drawing of the 3D plot. Naturally, it does arise in 2D. It is difficult to determine what is the most useful view for a particular plot without looking at it and experimenting with it; therefore, even if our final product is intended to be a file, a common workflow is to first create the plot using an interactive terminal (`x11` or `wxt`). Then we rotate the plot with the mouse, and possibly scale and zoom it using the middle mouse button, until we arrive at the desired appearance. This is what we mean by the comment in the `set view` command. Now we can reset the terminal to the final output device that we need, specify the output file, and simply say `replot`. The `view` and scaling at which we left the interactive plot is retained as a set of global settings and will be reflected in our final output file. These settings are also displayed at the bottom of the interactive plot window, so we can record them if we are going to make similar plots in the future, or want a set of plots to be drawn with the same settings. Note that we also redefined the `ztics` value. This is because when the plot is tilted to the final view angle that we chose, the perspective causes the tic labels on the vertical axis to be crowded together; this is a common problem with 3D plots, and taking manual control of the tics on the z-axis is the solution.

There's more...

Following is the same plot with one setting changed (aside from a slight adjustment in view angle):

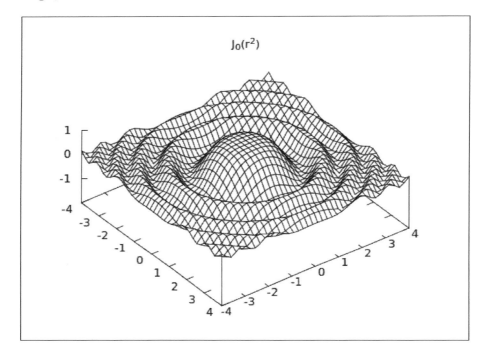

While the first plot was essentially a wireframe that we could see through, this version has the appearance of a solid, opaque surface. All we need to do is to say `set hidden3d`. This, which only works when `lines` or `linespoints` are being used, makes the surface appear opaque by removing from the plot any part of the surface, other surfaces, and other plot elements such as the axes and tic labels, that are behind the surface from our point of view. The underside of the surface is shown in a contrasting color with a color output device, but the two sides of the surface are not distinguished in monochrome. The name of the setting refers to the technique of **hidden line removal**; gnuplot is justly famed for the quality of its hidden line removal algorithm, and is one reason this program is so well regarded for its 3D plotting ability.

Using coordinate mappings

It is possible, when making 3D plots from data files, for the data to be interpreted in spherical or cylindrical coordinates rather than the default Cartesian system. For details, type `help set mapping`. We will give an example of using the cylindrical mapping to conveniently draw a shape with cylindrical symmetry.

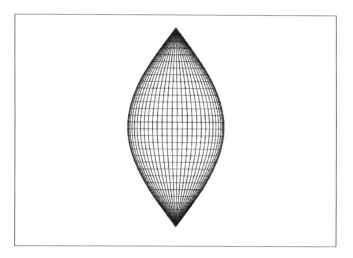

The previous figure is a perspective view of a surface that somewhat resembles a Christmas tree ornament. The relevant feature of this surface is that it has rotational symmetry around the z (vertical) axis, which means that it is most naturally expressed in cylindrical coordinates.

How to do it...

Try the following script:

```
set mapping cylindrical
unset tics
unset border
set hidden
set xrange [-pi : pi]
set yrange [-pi : pi]
set zrange [0 : pi]
set iso 60
unset key
splot '++' using 1:2:(sin($2)) with lines
```

How it works...

There are several new ideas used in this recipe. Breaking it down, these are:

The set mapping command

The first, highlighted line contains the new command that is the subject of this recipe. When the default Cartesian (*x-y-z*) coordinate system is changed to `cylindrical` then the columns of data read in during a data plot are interpreted as θ-z-r, where θ is the angular coordinate, z is the vertical coordinate, and r is the radius. A spherical mapping is also available and explained in the gnuplot online help (`help set mapping`). If the data file only has two columns, then the plot is drawn with r = 1.

In our example we don't want to plot from a data file, however. We want to plot a function given directly in the script. This presents us with a problem, as gnuplot does not support cylindrical or spherical plots of functions in 3D. The solution is to use one of gnuplot's **pseudofiles**.

The ++ pseudofile

These special files were introduced in *Chapter 1, Plotting Curves, Boxes, Points, and more*, where we learned how to use the "+" pseudofile for plotting functions in 2D using styles that are only available for data plots.

Here we turn to the 3D version. The "++" pseudofile creates rows of imaginary data with three columns *x-y-z* unless we change the coordinate mapping, which of course in this example we have. Setting the mapping to cylindrical means that the fictitious data columns will be interpreted as θ-z-r.

Now to plot a function, we use the `using` notation applied to the imaginary columns of data. We've done this in the final line of the script, where we plot the sine of the second column (z).

To clarify the use of "++" when plotting surfaces, note that, in Cartesian coordinates, the two commands

```
splot sin(x)+cos(y)
```

and

```
splot '++' using 1:2:(sin($1)+cos($2)) with lines
```

produce exactly the same plot.

Coordinate ranges

We have also established ranges for all variables in the `set xrange` and two other commands following it. The ranges for the polar coordinates are taken from the corresponding Cartesian coordinates, that is, when we set the xrange, we are setting both the range of the *x*-axis displayed on the plot *and* the range of the variable θ in the cylindrical coordinate system. It is mandatory to set `xrange` and `yrange` when using the "++" filename.

This mixing of the coordinate system in which the function is calculated and the Cartesian system in which it is displayed can be confusing, but the example shows a strategy, which should make it possible to get predictable results. Setting the `xrange` and `yrange` as we've done puts the r = 0 point in the middle of the graph and prevents part of the plot from being cut off. It also sets up a full rotation of the angular coordinate over a range of 2 π.

If we wanted to plot, say, our shape with half of it sliced off by a vertical plane, the easiest way to do this is not to fiddle with the coordinate ranges, but to apply a transformation to one of the fictitious data columns: `splot '++' using ($1/2):2:(sin($2))` with lines, will do the trick without any surprising side effects. In this example the underlying angular coordinate (column 1) still passes through a full rotation, but we've divided it in half without changing the way the figure is projected onto the Cartesian display. Note that the 60 isolines will still be used in our reduced angular range, so we might want to `set iso` to a smaller value.

Completing the picture

We've eliminated all of the graph adornments (`unset tics, unset border, unset key`) so we will be left with only the surface. The `isosamples` are set to give a sufficiently smooth surface drawing that is nevertheless not too crowded with isosurface lines (see the previous recipe). `set hidden` ensures that we shall see only the outer surface of the shape.

Coloring the surface

The wireframe `splot` with hidden line removal that we covered in the first recipe of this chapter, *Making a surface plot,* gives the visual impression of a solid surface. The numerical value encoded into the surface's height can be visually estimated, roughly, by the perspective provided by the isolines in conjunction with the tics on the vertical axis. But gnuplot also has a way to draw real solid surfaces whose height is indicated by color or shade.

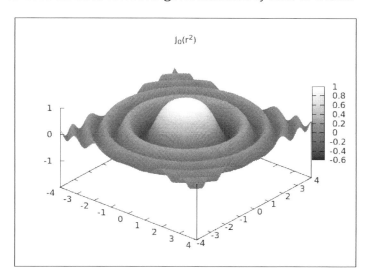

The previous figure shows the same mathematical function plotted in the first recipe in this chapter (*Making a surface plot*). Now the numerical value of the function at any point is indicated by both the height of the surface and its shade; the surface is now drawn as an opaque membrane rather than as a network of curves.

How to do it...

To produce the previous figure, run the following in gnuplot:

```
set isosamples 100
set samples 100
unset key
set title "J_0(r^2)"
set xrange [-4:4]
set yrange [-4:4]
set ztics 1
unset surface
set pm3d
splot besj0(x**2+y**2)
```

The surface will be drawn with a palette of colors when a color output device is being used and with a grayscale palette when using a monochrome terminal.

How it works...

If you compare the previous script with the one in the *Making a surface plot* recipe at the beginning of this chapter, you will see that the only significant difference is the highlighted line. The pm3d mode colors the imaginary surface being plotted according to its height or z-value at every point, with the mapping between the height and the color or shade determined by the **palette**, which we shall discuss in some more detail shortly.

The other modifications are to increase the number of isolines, in order to get a smoother surface, and to turn off the drawing of the individual isolines themselves with the command unset surface. We also need to set the sample frequency; generally we want this to be equal to the isosample frequency. In pm3d mode, the two orthogonal sets of isolines are drawn with two different spacings given by the two parameters. Although the gnuplot manual claims that the global hidden3d setting does not affect pm3d surface plots, it in fact seems to, and should not be turned on, as it appears to slightly degrade the drawing quality.

There's more...

Sometimes we want both a colored surface and a set of isolines; in fact, this can often be the clearest type of quantitative 3D plot. The way to achieve the highest quality in this type of graph is to use the hidden3d linestyle option to pm3d, as we do in the following script:

```
set iso 30
set samp 30
unset key
set title "J_0(r^2)"
set xrange [-4:4]
set yrange [-4:4]
set ztics 1
unset surf
set style line 1 lt 4 lw .5
set pm3d at s hidden3d 1
splot besj0(x**2+y**2)
```

This requires us to define a user linestyle, something we covered in *Chapter 3, Applying Colors and Styles*. Then the linestyle is referred to in an option to the set pm3d command. This will cause the isolines to be drawn using lines in this style, which allows us to have them in any color, thickness, or pattern supported by our terminal. Further, the isolines will be drawn with hidden line removal, so they will appear to be embedded in the opaque surface. As before, the global hidden3d option should not be turned on.

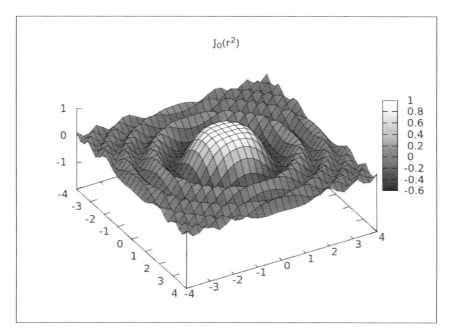

Note that we've also reduced the sample and isoline frequency, to keep our plot from being too crowded with isolines. (The `at s` component of the `set pm3d` command means *at surface*; this will become clearer later in the chapter.)

Making a contour plot

A **contour** plot is a set of **isolines**, or curves where the function or data has a constant value, drawn in the plane of the independent variables (*x* and *y* in Cartesian coordinates). It is simpler than the surface plots covered in the previous recipes in that it doesn't require the interpretation of perspective or hidden line removal. As there is no *z* axis for reference, the value that each isoline represents is represented by an individual label or by giving each line its own dash pattern or color.

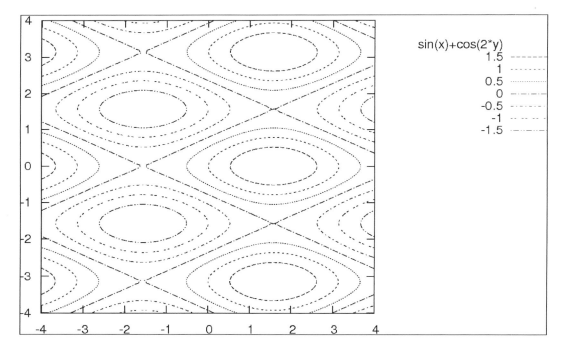

Certain types of patterns are better represented as surfaces, while for others, contours bring out more of the relevant characteristics. The rotationally invariant function that we plotted in the previous recipes in this chapter would yield a set of uninteresting circular contours; its structure is better conveyed by a surface plot. Here, we've plotted a function whose contour plot shows a pattern of nodal lines.

How to do it...

The following code sample will get you a contour plot:

```
set cntrparam levels 10
set contour base
unset sur
set view map
set xrange [-4:4]
set yrange [-4:4]
set iso 100
set samp 100
set key rmargin
splot sin(x)+cos(2*y)
```

How it works...

The number of contour lines drawn and which levels they follow are set with the `set cntrparam` command. The first command in the script asks for 10 automatically spaced levels; the number of levels we specify will actually be used by the program as an estimate of the number of levels it should actually use, not an exact number. We can also specify exactly which contour levels to use, rather than letting gnuplot calculate a set of automatic levels; see the online help for an exhaustive description of your options.

The second highlighted command tells gnuplot that our next `splot` command should draw a contour plot, and that the contour lines should be drawn on the base of the axis system, which is the *x-y* plane. As we want a contour plot only, without a surface plot as well, we need to say `unset sur[face]`, because the default behavior of the `splot` command is to draw a surface, as in the previous recipes.

The `set view map` command is a special option to the `set view` command that we saw previously. It rotates the coordinate system so that we are looking straight down from above, and is generally what we want for basic contour or image plots that shouldn't also incorporate surfaces.

As before, we need to set both the `isosamples` and the `samples` to get the desired number of contour lines in each direction. We place the legend, which will contain a key mapping each contour level to a color or dash pattern, on the right margin.

While many output terminals will produce a nice colored contour plot, if you need to create a monochrome plot using dash patterns to distinguish the contour levels, as shown in the paper version of this book, then you need to use the postscript terminal. The output file can then be easily converted to PNG or any other desired graphics format. But the other terminals, such as pngcairo, generally are not capable of producing high-quality (or any) dashed contours directly.

There's more...

Although we should be cautious about putting too much information on a plot, lest our graph become an indecipherable jumble of lines and curves, it is possible, with care, to combine contour and surface grid plots to produce a reasonable illustration such as the following:

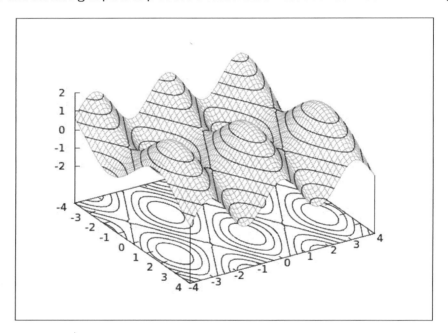

This is a plot of the same function as shown previously, with a contour plot on the base, a surface, and another set of contours drawn on the surface. Here is the script:

```
set iso 50
set samp 50
set yrange [-4:4]
set xrange [-4:4]
set ztics 1
```

```
unset key
set style line 1 linecolor rgb '#cccccc'
set contour both
set cntrparam levels 10
set hidd
splot sin(x)+cos(2*y) with lines linestyle 1
```

We've defined a line style having a light gray color and used it in the `splot` command. This is so that the grid lines forming the surface will be easily distinguishable from the contour lines. The latter will be drawn in various colors or, as shown, where a monochrome output terminal was used, as dark lines. The view angle was adjusted interactively for this plot.

Making a vector plot

When the quantity that depends on x and y has both magnitude and a direction it can be represented by an arrow whose length is proportional to the magnitude. The *x-y* plane can be broken into a regular grid and an arrow drawn in the plane, representing the direction and magnitude associated with each point on the grid—a **vector plot**. As we are associating two quantities, the magnitude and direction, or, equivalently, Δx and Δy, for each *x-y* pair, we can think of this type of plot as a 4D plot.

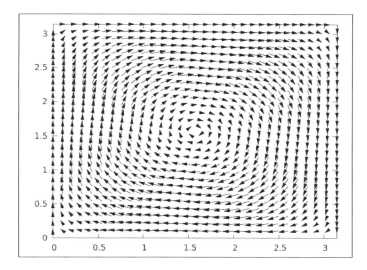

The previous figure is a vector field of a rotating flow. The exact appearance of the arrows will vary with the output terminal.

How to do it...

The following script draws the vector plot in the previous figure:

```
set xrange [0:pi]
set yrange [0:pi]
set iso 20
set samp 20
unset key
a = .2
plot '++' using 1:2:(-a*sin($1)*cos($2)):(a*cos($1)*sin($2))\
          w vec size  .06, 15 filled
```

How it works...

Vector plots require a data file or equivalent pseudofile. Four columns are used for x, y, Δx, and Δy. Our plot command uses a variable that we defined in the line above it, defines the four columns using gnuplot's `using` math syntax for manipulating column data and, in the highlighted section, asks for a vector plot. The `size` specification sets the `arrowstyle`. The first number is the length of the arrowhead and the second is the angle of the sides of the arrowhead in degrees. `filled` means to draw solid arrowheads. For all the details of how you can specify exactly how you want your vector arrows to look, say `help arrowstyle` at the gnuplot interactive prompt.

There's more...

gnuplot has the ability to plot a vector field on a surface, similarly to how it can plot contours on a surface, as we saw in the previous section.

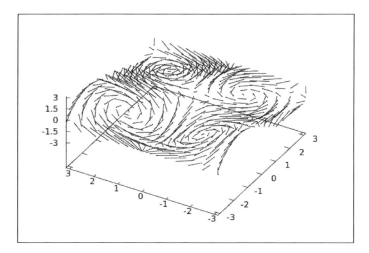

The vectors are plotted on an imaginary surface that is not depicted explicitly. Experimentation shows that the arrowstyle cannot be changed by the user, despite the documentation, but depends only on the terminal. This type of plot can be used, for instance, to describe a fluid flow in 3D; the contrived example shown was chosen to make the script easy to understand:

```
set xrange [-pi:pi]
set yrange [-pi:pi]
set zrange [-pi:pi]
unset key
set iso 20
set samp 20
set ztics 1.5
set view 37,300
a = .9
splot '++' using 1:2:(2*a*cos($2)*sin($1)):\
    (-a*sin($1)*cos($2)):(a*cos($1)*sin($2)):(a*cos($1)) w vec
```

The difference is the use of the `splot` command to create the vector plot rather than the `plot` command used previously for the planar vector plot. This requires six columns of data (or pseudo data): x, y, z, Δx, Δy, and Δz.

Making an image plot or heat map

The information that is presented in a planar contour plot can also be conveyed by coloring or shading the x-y plane, rather than by drawing contours on it. The resulting graph is called an **image plot**, or sometimes, a **heat map**:

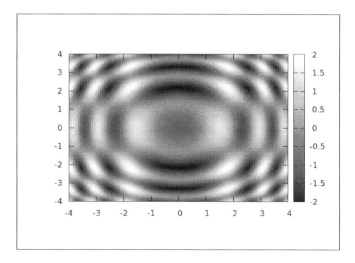

Depending on the character of the data to be plotted and the features one wants to call attention to, and to some extent the physical characteristics of the output device, either a contour plot or an image plot might be preferred.

How to do it...

The previous figure was created using the following script:

```
set xrange [-4:4]
set yrange [-4:4]
set iso 100
set samp 100
unset key
unset sur
set view map
set pm3d at b
splot sin(y**2+x**2) - cos(x**2)
```

How it works...

Let's look at the highlighted code line first. This `set pm3d` line, which we used at the beginning of the chapter to plot surfaces, here has the additional clause `at b`, which means *at bottom*. This says to draw the data color map on the *x-y* plane rather than on the surface itself. The line above it, which we also used before when learning how to make a contour plot, sets the view so that we are facing the *x-y* plane. With these preparations, the `splot` command creates an image plot using the default color palette. This palette is what defines the mapping from data value to color (or to gray value for monochrome terminals, as in the figure prepared for the printed version of this book). Note also that we've bumped up the isoline and sample frequency (we must do both again, one for each direction) for a smooth image plot. The line `unset sur[face]` is required to tell `splot` not to draw the surface itself, which would put a distracting grid of lines on top of our image plot.

There's more...

If we are using a color output device we may want to use something other than the default rainbow palette. gnuplot provides several different mechanisms for setting the palette, providing enough flexibility to specify any mapping we might require.

If we decide not to display the palette scale, the legend that shows the mapping from data values to colors, we need to use the following command:

```
unset colorbox
```

gnuplot allows us to read color tables from files or to define them with arbitrary mathematical functions that map from data value to each of the components of several available color spaces (RGB, and so on). There is even a library of predefined mathematical functions to choose from. But all this is fairly arcane and, in practice, we almost always want a linear interpolation between two or three specified colors in order to define a simple spectrum. Fortunately, gnuplot makes it very easy to do this. A few examples should make the method clear:

To get a spectrum that goes from black to gold, just give the command:

```
set palette defined (0 'black', 1 'gold')
```

The colors themselves can be specified using named colors, as we did here (try typing show colornames at the interactive prompt to see the list of over 100 names and their RGB values) or with the familiar #RRGGBB syntax, or in any other gnuplot-approved way.

If we decide we would like another color in the middle of the spectrum, we can try:

```
set palette defined (0 'black', 1 'aquamarine', 2 'gold')
```

Note that the actual numbers are not important; gnuplot rescales them to the interval [0,1] and interpolates between them, where 0 would be black and 1 would be white if we were plotting in grayscale.

Sometimes we want a sharp break somewhere in the palette to highlight a particular data value; this has the effect of combining a contour with the image map. To do this, we repeat a value:

```
set palette defined (0 'black', 1 'aquamarine', 1 'red', 2 'gold')
```

This will create a sharp transition in the palette between aquamarine and red, exactly in the middle of the range. The lower half of the palette will be a smooth transition from black to aquamarine, and the upper half will go smoothly from red to gold. We can define any number of these transitions, and create palettes of limitless complexity with this syntax.

Two more notes on mapping data to colors: If the data is better visualized with a logarithmic mapping rather than the default linear one, enter the set logscale cb command. To change the limits of the mapping, analogous to setting the *z* range, do set cbrange [a : b].

Combining contours and images

Sometimes we would like to plot two related but different sets of data on the same graph. In the case of 2D plots, it's simple: we just plot any number of curves and identify them with labels or a legend. But with 3D plots, trying to interpret a graph containing two different surfaces or sets of contours would be difficult, and plotting two heat maps simultaneously would not make any sense.

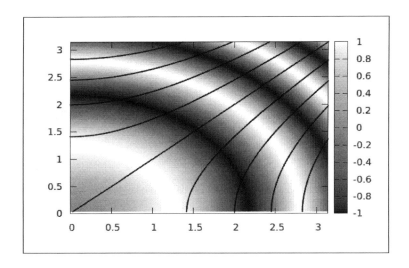

The previous figure shows one way to do this: plot contours and an image map together.

How to do it...

Feed this code to gnuplot to get the previous figure:

```
set xrange [0:pi]
set yrange [0:pi]
set iso 100
set samp 100
set cntrparam levels 10
unset key
unset surface
set view map
set contour base
set pm3d at b
splot '++' using 1:2:($1**2-$2**2):(sin($1**2+$2**2))\
    with lines lw 2
```

How it works...

We set everything up as in the previous contour plot example, but we also put in a `set pm3d at base`, so we are asking for both a contour plot and a colored surface plot. How do we make the surface, which will appear as an image plot here, and the contours to represent distinct sets of data? The `splot` command, when plotting data from a file or the "++" pseudofile, can take an optional fourth column. When this is present, it will be used to color the surface, which itself, as before, will be defined by the third column. This can be used to draw a surface in 3D perspective view, which is colored to represent some related quantity, rather than to redundantly indicate its height. Or, as here, it can be used to draw contours over a "surface" that is rendered as an image map. The function for the contours is given in the third column, which, using coordinate variables rather than the columns' index's, is `x**2 - y**2`, and the fourth column defines the image map: `sin(x**2 + y**2)`.

Combining surfaces with images

It is possible to plot a surface and its projection as a color image on the *x-y* plane on the same graph. The two simultaneous views of the same data or function can be useful to bring out the topography of a complex surface.

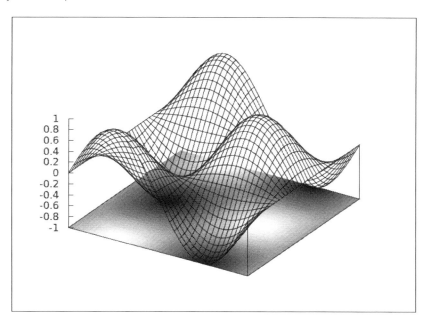

The previous figure shows a simple trigonometric function of two variables displayed as a surface with its values simultaneously encoded into colors (or gray values) at the base of the plot.

How to do it...

The following script produces the previous figure as its output:

```
set iso 40
set samp 40
unset key
set xrange [-pi:pi]
set yrange [-pi:pi]
f(x,y) = sin(x)*cos(y)
set hidden front
set xyplane at -1
splot f(x,y) with pm3d at b, f(x,y) with lines
```

How it works...

The new features we are combining to produce this graph are in the highlighted lines in the code sample. Let's look at the last command first. The first part of the `splot` command plots the function f(), which is defined three lines above, as a colored surface at the **base** of the plot; this is what `pm3d at b` does. The second part, after the comma, plots the function again, without `pm3d` but `with lines`. This plots the wireframe surface.

The function varies from -1 to 1, but we want it to lie completely above the base upon which the surface is drawn, so we need to change the z value at which we place the base. This is the purpose of the second to last line.

Finally, we would like the surface to appear solid. But when combining surfaces with `pm3d` color plots, we need to add an extra option to the `set hidden3d` command, because the hidden line removal does not apply to the `pm3d` part of the graph. The command `set hidden front` tells gnuplot to draw the parts of the graph involving the hidden line removal procedure after the other parts, so they appear to be "in front" of the colored base, giving the effect we want.

There's more...

We can make the image intersect the surface, as shown in the following:

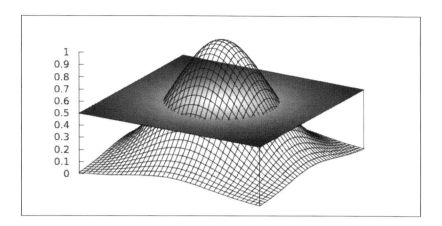

This is a simple 2D Gaussian surface cut through by the *x-y* plane, upon which the function's values are shown as colors or in grayscale. The code follows:

```
set samp 40
set iso 40
set yrange [-1.5:1.5]
set xrange [-1.5:1.5]
unset ytics
unset xtics
unset key
unset colorbox
set hidden3d front
a = .5
set xyplane at a
f(x,y) = exp(-x**2-y**2)
splot f(x,y) with pm3d at b, f(x,y) with lines, a with lines lt -100
```

We've taken advantage of the fact that we can place the base wherever we want to make it intersect the surface at a, which we've set to `0.5`. But it's not quite so simple, as a little trick is required to make the color projection on the base to appear to be opaque; otherwise, we would be able to see the surface through it, which would make the graph confusing. Remember that hidden line removal does not work on the `pm3d` surface, so we need to add something else to the *x-y* plane to make it appear to be opaque. This is the purpose of the last part of the `splot` command, where we have asked for a plot of the constant value a using the linetype (`lt`) `-100`. As the global `hidden3d` option is turned on, this plot will be made using hidden line removal; and as we have specified a linetype that happens not to exist, the lines themselves will be invisible. The net result is a surface, invisible except for its ability to hide what is beneath it, having the constant value a, which will exactly coincide with the base of the plot.

We can also plot two different sets of data or functions, one used for the surface and the other for the image:

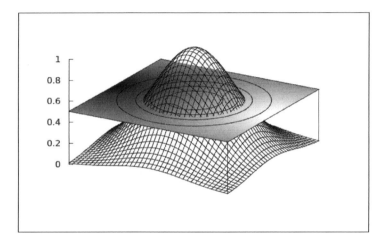

The previous plot retains the 2D Gaussian surface from before but plots a simple 2D trigonometric function in an image. For good measure, we've thrown in a contour plot as well. The plot was made with the following script:

```
set samp 40
set iso 40
set yrange [-1.5:1.5]
set xrange [-1.5:1.5]
set zrange [0:1]
unset ytics
unset xtics
unset key
unset colorbox
```

```
set hidden3d front
a = .5
set xyplane at a
set contour base
f(x,y) = exp(-x**2-y**2)
splot '++' using 1:2:(a):(sin($1)*cos($2)) with pm3d at b,\
       '++' using 1:2:(f($1,$2)) with lines, a with lines lt -100
```

By now, this should all be familiar, except for the last command. We've combined our previous tricks with the use of the "++" pseudofile in order to get different data used for the surface (and contours) and the image. This is the technique used earlier in this chapter in the *Combining contours and images* recipe.

Plotting a path in 3D

Back in *Chapter 1, Plotting Curves, Boxes, Points, and more,* we used parametric plotting to make graphs of complicated 2D paths. We can do the same thing in 3D to draw a complex curve in space.

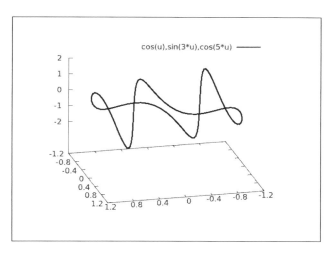

This might be thought of as a 3D Lissajous figure. The path intersects itself at several places.

How to do it...

Following is the code for the previous figure:

```
set samp 100
set xtics .4
set ytics .4
set parametric
```

```
set urange [-pi:pi]
set ztics 1
splot cos(u),sin(3*u),cos(5*u) lw 2
```

Note that the appearance of the plot will change radically depending on the viewpoint.

How it works...

In exploring parametric plotting in 2D in *Chapter 1, Plotting Curves, Boxes, Points, and more*, we learned that the x and y independent variables were replaced by the single parameter t, and we had to specify two functions separated by commas; the first gave the x coordinate and the second gave the y coordinate that were plotted simultaneously as t was varied between the limits defined in the trange.

To plot a parametric curve in 3D, it may not come as a surprise that we need to specify three functions (or data columns) separated by commas. This can be seen in the last command of the previous script. When we give the command set parametric in 3D, two new independent variables u and v are established, which act as the parameters. We need to set their ranges, which we do here with the set urange command (we don't use v in this example, but we do in the next, when we explore parametric surfaces).

Drawing parametric surfaces

gnuplot allows us to define surfaces parametrically, which allows us to plot complex and possibly self-intersecting shapes.

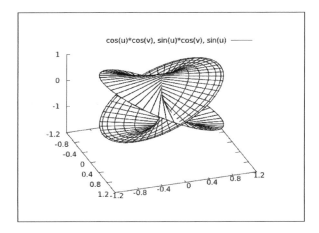

The previous figure shows a surface that slices through itself in 3D.

How to do it...

Following is the script for the previous figure:

```
set param
set iso 50
set ztics .5
set xtics .4
set ytics .4
set urange [-pi:pi]
set vrange [-pi:pi]
set hidd
splot cos(u)*cos(v), sin(u)*cos(v), sin(u)
```

How it works...

As in the previous recipe, we provide the x, y, and z components, but the provision of components that depend on both parameters (u and v) defines a surface rather than merely a path through the 3D space.

There's more...

The same thing can be done with colored surfaces.

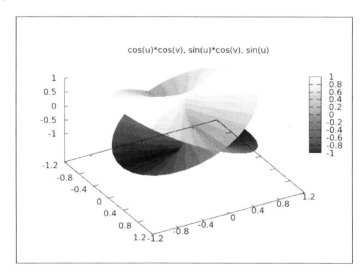

The previous figure is of the same function that we plotted in the one prior to it, rendered as a color-coded surface rather than a wireframe. Note that although the axes are visible through the surface, the surface is hidden by itself. Following is the script that produced the previous figure:

```
set param
set iso 50
set ztics .5
set xtics .4
set ytics .4
set urange [-pi:pi]
set vrange [-pi:pi]
set pm3d depthorder
splot cos(u)*cos(v), sin(u)*cos(v), sin(u) with pm3d
```

We've added something to the splot command with pm3d. We also set a special pm3d option with set pm3d depthorder. This option causes gnuplot to draw the surface starting with the elements farthest away from our viewpoint, which simulates hidden line removal and renders the surface as if it were opaque, making it much easier to understand visually.

9
Using and Making Graphical User Interfaces

This chapter contains the following recipes:

- ▶ Using the JAVA gnuplot GUI JGP
- ▶ Using the Emacs GUI
- ▶ Sharing with Plotshare
- ▶ Writing a web GUI for gnuplot

Introduction

The tremendous utility and flexibility of gnuplot is due in large part to its essential nature as a command-line program. This allows it to be controlled by scripts or with text sent through a pipe or socket, which opens up an unlimited horizon of interoperability. gnuplot can be used from within any programming language, using either a custom interface or through the general method of writing to a socket. Indeed, it is the flexibility of a textual interface that is largely responsible for the enduring popularity of gnuplot among programmers, scientists, and other demanding technical users.

However, there are milieus for which it can be an advantage or a requirement to wed the superior technical graphing abilities of gnuplot with a graphical user interface or **GUI**. Some of these situations might include using gnuplot as a back end for an interactive web page that produces graphs in response to user input. We might also want to make gnuplot output available to people who use it infrequently and are therefore unfamiliar with its options, but need some graphs quickly.

In the latter case, a GUI front end to gnuplot might allow users to make sophisticated graphs without becoming experts or even having to consult a manual. There is undoubtedly a place for such aids, but the user who demands more control over the final result and the ability to work as efficiently as possible will of course buy this book and learn to use gnuplot's native command-line interface.

Using the Java gnuplot GUI JGP

In this recipe, we learn how to get started with the JGP program, which provides a basic but serviceable GUI front end to gnuplot.

Getting ready

JGP does not come with a normal gnuplot installation. You need to go to its home page at http://jgp.sourceforge.net/ and download the source code and Java binaries (JGP is an open source project, distributed under the GPL license, and authored by Maximilian Fabricius). You can compile it yourself or simply run the supplied binaries. The current version of the software works only with the Linux operating system. I encountered no difficulties running version 0.1.2 pre alpha of the software, using the Java binaries as supplied in the download. You should have Java version 5.0 installed, and in order for JGP to find gnuplot, it must be on your path.

Where is gnuplot?

To use GUI front ends, gnuplot must be on your path. For example, if you have been typing /usr/local/bin/gnuplot, you must now add this to your path with (using bash-type syntax) export PATH=$PATH:/usr/local/bin and put this command in your shell startup file.

How to do it...

It's pretty straightforward to get started with JGP. The following steps explain what you need to do:

1. Installing and starting up

After unzipping the downloaded archive, you should have a file called jgp. Make it executable, if it is not already, with the command chmod +x jgp. Then you can start the program by typing ./jgp.

The following screenshot shows you what it will look like after making a plot:

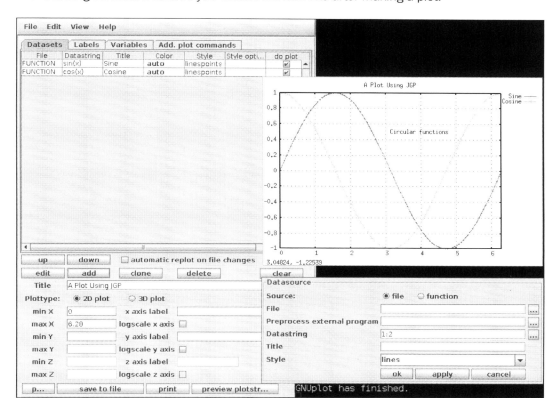

In the previous screenshot, we can see the main interface window, a plot output window, and another window that can be used for defining additional data sources or functions. The main (largest) window shows the functions that are plotted. We can also see a bit of the terminal window from which we started the program peeking out at the bottom. One quirk with JGP is that it must not be put in the background, but must be left in the foreground, so this terminal window cannot be used for any other purpose while JGP is running.

2. Doing more with JGP

There are separate windows for adding other features to the plot:

The previous screenshot shows the window that we used for adding the label **Circular functions**. These windows are accessed by clicking on the tabs that can be seen in the large main window.

We clicked on the tab **Add. plot commands** to get the window in the following screenshot:

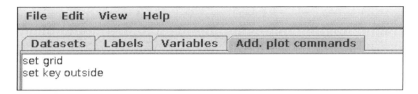

We used this to set the parameters for the key and the grid; this window is for adding commands to the plot script that are not directly accessible from the GUI.

Although a little rough around the edges, JGP certainly provides a usable GUI for gnuplot on Linux that less experienced users might appreciate. It also has the advantage of being, similar to gnuplot itself, open source software.

Using the Emacs GUI

Emacs is one of the two most venerable and powerful text editors used by programmers and other expert users of computing systems derived from the UNIX fork of computer history. While the other one, **Vim**, is of course superior, Emacs has the ability to be customized to such an extreme extent that it can be turned into a textual or even a graphical interface for other programs. There are Emacs modes for reading mail and netnews, playing games, and much more. In this recipe, we will introduce Emacs **gnuplot-mode**, which is a useful GUI for gnuplot.

Getting ready

Naturally, you need to have Emacs installed. Emacs comes in various flavors. You need one with hooks into your operating system's graphical libraries compiled in. If you are on Linux or Apple's OS X there is a good chance that you already have such a version of Emacs installed. Most versions of Emacs for Windows should also work. We mention this because there is a small chance that you might have a stripped down version that cannot support a GUI customization, in which case you will need to upgrade your Emacs before trying to use gnuplot-mode.

You will need to install gnuplot-mode using whatever method you use on your system to install Emacs modes. It is normally not installed by default. On Linux systems such as Ubuntu, it is packaged separately (and called "gnuplot-mode") by the system package manager. If all else fails you can download it from its github home at `https://github.com/bruceravel/gnuplot-mode/downloads`.

How to do it...

The gnuplot-mode editing mode for Emacs provides a handful of facilities that make writing gnuplot scripts more convenient. It offers syntax coloring, automatic completion of gnuplot keywords, automatic indentation, as well as a system of menus to help us when we forget how to do something in gnuplot. It includes its own interface into the gnuplot help system, too.

1. Running a gnuplot script

The following screenshot shows what we will see after we've written a script and executed it:

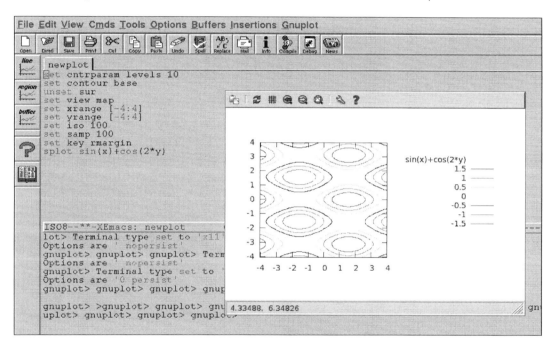

The big buttons on the left allow us to execute either the whole script or selected lines. After a plot command is executed, we get a new interactive window containing our graph.

2. Help and menus

The following screenshot illustrates some parts of the interface, showing a help screen and illustrating how we can use the menus to insert lines into our script:

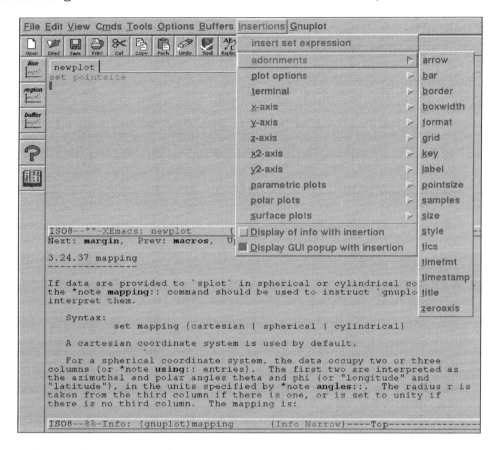

Sharing with Plotshare

This section will explain how to get graphs from gnuplot even if you don't have gnuplot installed.

How to do it...

Go to `http://www.plotshare.com/`. You will find a web page with a box near the top. Enter a gnuplot script in the box and click the **execute** button, and you will get the same result as if you had run the script through gnuplot on your own machine. You can even upload datafiles to be saved on the server and plotted.

In addition to providing graphing services, this website is designed so you can share your gnuplot scripts with others and work on them collaboratively. You can click on the **recent** tab to see the scripts and resulting output submitted by other users, which can be a fun and interesting way to learn about the program.

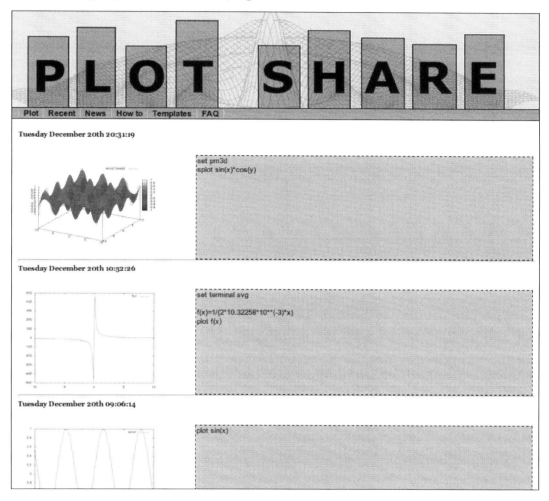

The previous screenshot shows what the **recent** section of the Plotshare website looks like.

How it works...

Because gnuplot is a C program with the ability to use the filesystem, execute system commands, and do other powerful and dangerous things, allowing it to execute arbitrary user commands would be a security nightmare, essentially handing control of the server over to the first malicious person with the requisite knowledge. For these reasons, there are a few limitations in the commands you can use in your scripts on Plotshare; for example, only the `png` terminal is allowed (and you can leave the `set term` command out, as it is the default, as well as the `set output` commands). There is a limit of 10 plotting commands in a script and some limits on resources consumed.

The people behind this project have generously donated a unique and extremely valuable resource to the community. One hopes that it is used responsibly, for exploration, sharing, and a reasonable amount of plot generation, and not abused.

Writing a web GUI for gnuplot

This final recipe will teach you how to make your own interactive web application that uses gnuplot to draw a graph in response to user input. It is not a general-purpose GUI for gnuplot as was the subject of the previous recipe, but rather shows one way to use gnuplot as part of a special-purpose web application. Because gnuplot can be controlled through text commands and can create PNG files, which are size-efficient and well supported by current web browsers, it is very well suited to this type of project.

We are going to create a simple game that asks the user to hit a target with a cannonball. The player enters two numbers, the initial speed of the projectile and the angle of the cannon. After clicking on a button labeled **fire!**, a graph is displayed showing the trajectory of the cannonball calculated from the two input numbers and plotted by gnuplot. The player can repeatedly enter new numbers and fire, and each time the graph will be replaced. The game can be used to illustrate the elementary principles of ballistics; there are an infinite number of correct solutions that can be calculated with simple physics (there are no advanced complications such as air resistance).

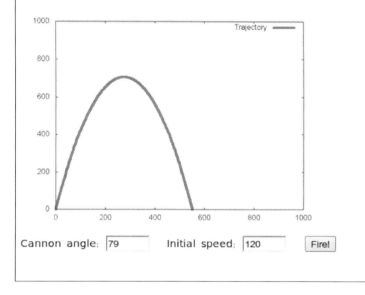

Aim the Cannonball

Enter values for the angle from the horizontal, in degrees, of the cannon, and the inital speed of the cannonball. Your goal is for the ball to hit the ground at x = 1,000 meters. Gravity is that of earth, 9.8 meters/second^2.

Cannon angle: 79   Initial speed: 120   Fire!

The previous figure shows what the game looks like; this is a screenshot taken directly from the browser window.

Getting ready

We need a few things in place in order to run a web application. Our example will use the Python scripting language for the back end, so we'll need to have a Python interpreter installed. Fortunately, this is very widespread and comes built-in on Macintosh OS X and many other systems; it's also free, open source, and easy to install. In order for Python code to run in response to requests from a web browser, we also need to install a Python web framework. There are plenty of these to choose from, and it doesn't really matter which one we choose, as our bare-bones application will be easily modified to use any of them. In order to give a specific working example, we chose the Django framework (`https://www.djangoproject.com/`), which is also open source and can be installed anywhere Python is installed. Nevertheless, there is nothing in our example that depends on any special features of Django.

How to do it...

The entire main application fits into one Python file. In the following steps we provide a listing of the main program, two short auxiliary files, and explain how to run the application:

1. The program

The following listing shows the main Python program:

```
from django.http import HttpResponse
import commands
c = commands.getoutput
GPATH = '/webapps/cannon/'
def draw(request):
    angle = request.POST.get('angle', "0")
    speed = request.POST.get('speed', "0")
    try:
        angle = float(angle)
        speed = float(speed)
    except:
        warning = """Enter numbers: the angle should be positive and
less than 90 degrees and the speed
                    must be positive."""
    else:
        if not ( 0<=angle<=90 and 0<=speed ):
            warning = """The angle should be positive and less than 90
degrees and the speed must be positive."""
            angle = "0"
            speed = "0"
        else:
            warning = ''
            gnuplotscript ='g = 9.8; a = %s; v = %s; set angle degrees;
set term png; set out "%scannongraph.png"; set parametric; set samp
5000; set trange [0:1000]; set yrange [0:1000]; set xrange [0:1000];
plot v*cos(a)*t, v*sin(a)*t-g/2.*t**2 lw 5 title "Trajectory"' %
(angle, speed, GPATH)
            c('gnuplot -e \'%s\'' % gnuplotscript)
    page = """
    <!DOCTYPE HTML>
    <head><meta content="text/html;charset=utf-8" http-equiv="Content-
Type">
    <title>Aim the Cannonball</title>
    </head><body>
    <h1>Aim the Cannonball</h1>
    <p style = "width:32em;">Enter values for the angle from the
horizontal, in degrees, of the cannon, and the inital speed of the
cannonball. Your goal is for the ball to hit the ground at x = 1,000
meters. Gravity is that of earth, 9.8 meters/second<sup>2</sup>.
    </p>
```

```
    <form name = "cannon" action = "/cannongraph/" method = "post">
     <img src = "/cannongraph.png" width= "400" /><br />
    Cannon angle: <input type = "text" size = "4" name = "angle" value
= "%s">  
    Initial speed: <input type = "text" size = "4" name="speed" value =
"%s">  
    <input type="submit" name = "fire" value = "Fire!" />
    </form>
    <p style = "color:red; width:32em;">%s</p>
    </body></html>
    """ % (angle, speed, warning)
    response = HttpResponse(page)
    response['Cache-Control'] = 'no-cache'
    return response
```

This file is supplied as `draw.py`. We need to choose a place to store the graph as well as the `draw.py` program and the associated project files that we describe later. We shall store the graph files in `/webapps/cannon/` and the program and project files in `webapps/cannon/`, which is not an absolute filesystem path but part of the directory tree rooted somewhere in Python's module loading path, so it can find and load these files (both paths might be the same if / is on the Python path; in Python we turn the filesystem path into a path for importing by placing `__init__.py` files in each directory in the chain).

2. The auxiliary files

The rest of the details in this recipe are most appropriate for deployment on a local machine. In order to connect the action `/cannongraph/` to the script, we need to route the URL, which is accomplished in Django with a `urls.py` file:

```
fromdjango.conf.urls.defaults import *
fromdjango.conf import settings
urlpatterns = patterns('',
   (r'^cannongraph/$', 'webapps.cannon.draw.draw'),
   (r'^(.*.png)/$', 'django.views.static.serve', {'document_root':
   settings.MEDIA_ROOT}),)
```

We also need a settings file:

```
DEBUG = True
TIME_ZONE = 'America/New_York'
LANGUAGE_CODE = 'en-us'
MEDIA_ROOT = '/webapps/cannon/'
MIDDLEWARE_CLASSES = ( "django.middleware.common.CommonMiddleware",)
ROOT_URLCONF = 'webapps.cannon.urls'
INSTALLED_APPS = ('webapps.cannon.draw',)
```

3. Running

Now, for use on our local machine, we need merely start Django's development server, setting an environment variable pointing to our settings file:

```
DJANGO_SETTINGS_MODULE=webapps.cannon.settings django-admin.py runserver
&
```

Some of the details regarding settings and URL dispatch, and especially the method of starting the local web server, will vary between web frameworks or libraries, but the main program in the file `draw.py` should be nearly independent of framework. Indeed, it is likely to be entirely portable between most frameworks aside from its very first and last lines (and possibly the `request.POST.get` statements).

Next, we fire up any reasonably modern web browser and navigate to `http://127.0.0.1:8000/cannongraph/`, and we should see the initial screen of our application. After entering some numbers and clicking on the **fire** button, we should see something similar to what is shown in the previous figure.

How it works...

The development server started by the `django-admin.py` program opens (by default) port 8000 on the local machine. This is pointed to by the URL `http://127.0.0.1:8000/`. The last component of the URL, `cannongraph/`, is looked up in the list of regular expressions in the file `urls.py`, where it is matched to `webapps.cannon.draw.draw`, which causes django to execute the function `draw` in the module `webapps.cannon.draw`, which in turn is the file `draw.py` in the Python path `webapps.cannon`. The `settings.py` file tells Django where to look for the `urls.py` file, and activates the `webapps.cannon.draw` module.

The `draw` function sets the angle and speed variables by attempting to read the appropriate entries from the `request.POST` dictionary, which is the dictionary of values sent by a form on a web page using the **POST** method. If there are no corresponding values in the dictionary, the fallback "0" values are assigned. Initially, when first navigating to the page, this dictionary is empty, because no form has been submitted yet, so these initial values are assigned. If there are values submitted, they are checked to ensure that they are within the appropriate ranges for the problem and that they are in fact numbers. If a service like this is deployed publicly, one must be sure, as mentioned in the previous recipe, not to trust user input. Even in a highly constrained situation such as the one in this example, where arbitrary scripts are not being sent to gnuplot, the inputs should be sanitized before being used.

If the submitted numbers are acceptable, then the variable `gnuplotscript` is defined. This is the script that will be sent to gnuplot, in the form of a single line with commands separated by semicolons. We will use it with the **-e** option to the gnuplot command, which accepts a script in this form on the command line.

After this, the `page` variable is set. This is a long string that holds the entire web page. It contains three locations where the variable's `speed`, `angle`, and `warning` are interpolated. Python's method of interpolating values into strings is so convenient that it makes the use of template languages unnecessary.

Note the `action` attribute of the `form` tag in the page. The value `/cannongraph/` submits the form to the URL `http://127.0.0.1:8000/cannongraph/` with the form input values sent along as POST data (determined by the form's **method** attribute). This is in turn looked up and dispatched by the table in `urls.py`, and we begin again.

The last line in the program sends the page to the browser as a properly formatted web response. We've set a response header to disable caching in the browser, to try to ensure that the user sees the newly calculated figure each time the form is submitted.

We have kept this example simple and bare-bones, in order to expose the structure of the project, as lucidly as possible while constructing a working web service that does something mildly interesting. In practice, there would be all sorts of graphics, JavaScript, other options, extra security checking, resource limiting, and more. But the general method can be elaborated upon in infinite ways to add interactive plotting capabilities to web applications.

10
Surveying Special Topics

This chapter contains the following recipes:

- ▶ Avoiding overlapping labels
- ▶ Plotting labels from files
- ▶ Mapping the Earth
- ▶ Making a labeled contour plot
- ▶ Softening the axes
- ▶ Putting arrows on the axes
- ▶ Plotting with pictures
- ▶ Breaking an axis
- ▶ Fitting the grid to the data
- ▶ Coloring the axes

Introduction

This chapter collects a few special topics that didn't quite fit anywhere else. Some of these are completely new topics and some are elaborations of examples from earlier chapters. All of them assume some familiarity with common gnuplot commands introduced elsewhere in the book.

Avoiding overlapping labels

We devote our first recipe in this chapter to demonstrating several ways to avoid a common problem with gnuplot. As mentioned in previous chapters, gnuplot does not really try to account for the horizontal space occupied by tic labels, simply placing them at the tic positions and printing them in the selected tic font, whether that is the default or the one specified by the user.

This works acceptably well most of the time, but can fail spectacularly if our labels are long or we've chosen a big font. In these cases, the tic labels on the x-axis are in danger of overlapping. This is a particularly common problem when gnuplot is used to generate graphs automatically, where the user has no opportunity to tune each graph by hand.

In this recipe, we'll explore two ways to deal with long x-axis labels that don't require the use of tiny fonts to squeeze them in. The following figure shows the use of some very long numerical labels that are rotated to get them to fit, in a fashion reminiscent of some parking space arrangements:

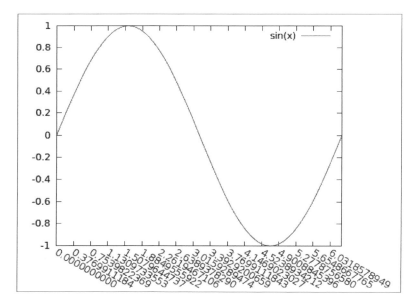

How to do it...

Feed the following script to gnuplot to produce the previous figure:

```
set xrange [0:2*pi]
set xtics 0, 0.12*pi, 2*pi
set xtics format "%.10f"
```

```
set xtics rotate by -30
set rmargin 10
plot sin(x)
```

How it works...

The first two lines should not contain any surprises. The third line tells gnuplot to print the tic labels on the x-axis with 10 places following the decimal point, which should take up a bit of room. The third line rotates the labels by 30 degrees clockwise from the axis. We then need to increase the margin on the right of the graph to avoid cutting off the labels near the right, which is what the `set rmargin` command accomplishes.

There's more...

The problem of long labels often arises when we are plotting dates and times (see *Chapter 4, Controlling your Tics*). gnuplot tries to avoid collisions by truncating date/time tic labels at 24 characters. This is unfortunate, because it not only fails to solve the problem but severely constrains the format of our labels.

If we try the following settings followed by any plot command, then we get the figure that follows, where the labels overlap:

```
set xdata time
set format x "%A, %b %d, %Y"
set xrange ["1/1/72" : "1/10/72"]
```

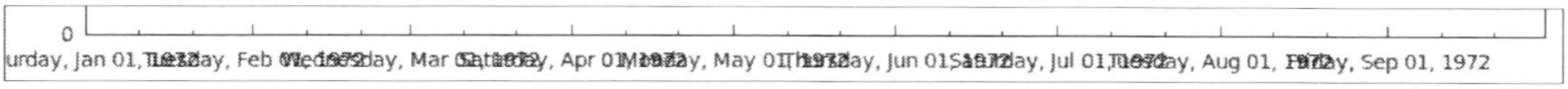

These commands tell gnuplot that we're working with time/date data, that our label format should follow the pattern "Thursday, Jan 26, 2012", and that the range along the x-axis should cover 10 days starting at Jan 1, 1972.

We can fix this with one change to the format:

```
set format x "%A\n%b %d, %Y"
```

The previous command inserts a linebreak (\n) after the code for the weekday, leading to the arrangement of labels on the axis shown in the following figure:

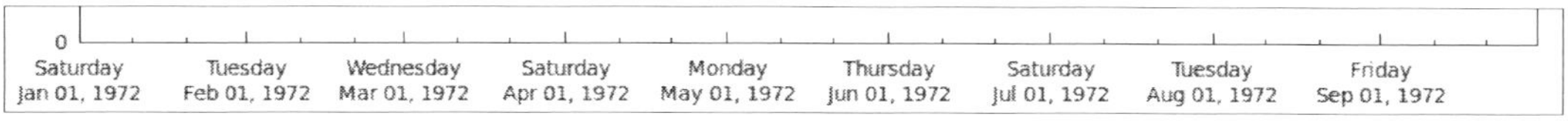

Plotting labels from files

In *Chapter 2, Annotating with Labels and Legends*, we learned how to place a text label anywhere on the graph with the `set label` command. It is also possible to plot a set of labels whose text, positions, and possibly other attributes are derived from the information in a datafile. In this way, we can create visualizations such as the following:

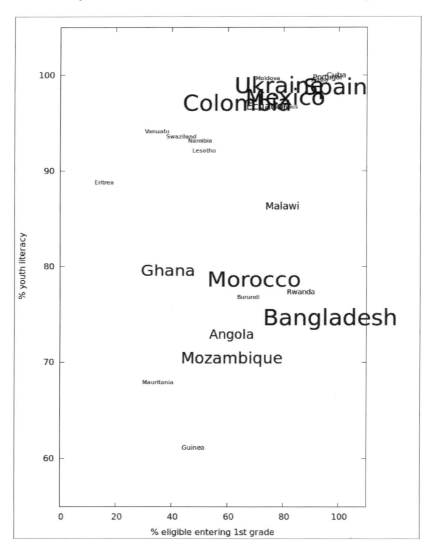

The previous figure shows a collection of names of countries printed with a text size that is proportional to each country's population (aside from the practical requirement to impose a maximum and minimum font size). The labels are positioned to indicate each country's school intake rate in the first grade as a percentage of official school-age population versus the literacy rate for people in the age group 15-24. The data comes from the World Bank and can be found at `http://data.worldbank.org/data-catalog/world-development-indicators`. The numbers reported for 2009 are used, and all countries with data for that year are plotted.

Getting ready

We are going to read in data from the file `p3.dat`, which is provided with this book.

How to do it...

Execute the following gnuplot script to produce the previous figure:

```
set term pngcairo enhanced size 750, 1000
set out 'p3.png'
unset key
set rmargin 10
set xrange [0:110]
set yrange [55:105]
set xlabel '% eligible entering 1st grade'
set ylabel '% youth literacy'
min(a,b) = (a<b?a:b)
max(a,b) = (a>b?b:a)
scale(x) = min(max(x/1000000,8), 32)
CountryName(String,Size) = sprintf("{/=%d %s}", scale(Size), String)
plot 'p3.dat' using 2:3:(CountryName(stringcolumn(1),$4)) with labels
```

How it works...

Since we are going to be using codes to set the font size for each label, we need to select a terminal that supports enhanced text, which is the purpose of the first line of the script. We've also set a size that will help keep our labels from becoming too crowded together; this was chosen through trial-and-error.

A text legend on this type of plot would just be confusing, so we've turned it off with `unset key`. We've increased the size of the right margin to make room for one of the labels that sticks out.

The next two lines that require some explanation are the definitions of the `min` and `max` functions. gnuplot does not come with these, so we had to make our own. We've used the ternary operator explained in *Chapter 7, Programming gnuplot and Dealing with Data* to very simply create functions that return the minimum or maximum of two arguments, which is all that we'll need them to do.

After that we've defined a `scale` function that uses our min and max functions. This function transforms the large population numbers to much smaller font sizes, and imposes minimum and maximum font size cutoffs. The particular numbers used were arrived at largely through trial and error.

The `CountryName` function takes two arguments. The first will be the name of the country read from the file. The second will be a size, which we will read in from the column giving the total population. The `CountryName` function inserts the enhanced text code for setting the font size, which it calculates using our scale function.

Finally, the `plot` command in the last line uses the `labels` style. This style accepts three entries for the *x* and *y* coordinates and the text to be positioned at those coordinates (it is also possible to plot labels in 3D). We use the `stringcolumn` function here, which returns, as a string, the text of the column given in its argument.

The general approach in this recipe is inspired by the example provided in the online help under `help labels`.

Mapping the Earth

The main purpose of this recipe is to call attention to the fact that gnuplot comes with a very useful datafile called `world.dat`. This consists of coordinates for a rough outline of the Earth's land masses, as latitude and longitude in the usual degree units. It can be used as a map background for plotting other geographically relevant data. In the following figure, we've overlaid some data on recent earthquake activity:

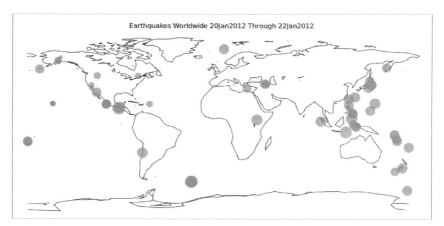

Getting ready

We've included a copy of the `world.dat` datafile in case you've mislaid the one that comes with gnuplot. You also need to have the file `earthquakes.dat`. This contains data from the United States Geological Survey and contains the locations, magnitudes, and other information about all the earthquakes in the world for three recent days. We've simply changed the format in which the latitudes and longitudes are recorded to make the data digestible by gnuplot. The S (South) and W (West) coordinates were turned into negative numbers and N (North) and E (East) coordinates were turned into unadorned positive numbers. You need to be in the same directory as these datafiles in order for the example script to work as written.

How to do it...

The following script will produce the earthquake map:

```
unset tics
unset border
unset key
set title "Earthquakes Worldwide 20Jan2012 Through 22Jan2012"
set style fill transparent solid 0.4 noborder
plot 'world.dat' with lines lt -1,\
     'earthquakes.dat' using 4:3:6 with circles
```

How it works...

We've seen all of these gnuplot commands in earlier chapters. Our map will look better without a border or a legend, so we do away with these adornments in the first three lines, and then set a title.

The `set style` line determines the style of the circles that we are going to plot to show the locations of the earthquakes. We want them to be filled with a partially transparent solid color (that we leave as the default) and to not have a border.

Finally, we plot from the two datafiles. The map data is plotted with solid black lines and the earthquake data is plotted with circles. The longitude is plotted along the horizontal coordinate and the latitude is plotted along the vertical coordinate; the latter is in the third column and the former is in the fourth column of the file. The third entry in the `using` clause will be used for the sizes of the circles; we've told gnuplot to use the sixth column, which contains the earthquake magnitudes.

Using partially transparent circles lets us see the map boundaries through them, and also makes it clear when two earthquakes occurred at the same position.

There's more...

We learned how to plot 3D data from files in spherical or cylindrical coordinates in the recipe *Using coordinate mappings*, in *Chapter 8, The Third Dimension*. We can use this technique to make a globe of the Earth from the `world.dat` data:

The previous figure was produced by loading the following script into gnuplot:

```
set mapping spherical
set angles degrees
set isosamples 30
set xrange [-1:1]
set yrange [-1:1]
unset tics
unset border
set parametric
set hidden3d
set urange [-90:90]
set vrange [0:360]
unset key
splot cos(u)*cos(v),cos(u)*sin(v),sin(u) with lines lt rgb '#dddddd',\
      'world.dat' with lines lt -1
```

We learned about the `set Mapping` command in *Chapter 8, The Third Dimension*. We need to set the angles to degrees to use latitudes and longitudes directly on the sphere. The `set parametric` command does not affect the plot of land masses from the datafile, but it does allow us a convenient way to express a set of latitude and longitude lines covering the globe. The `splot` command in the last line uses a common parametric representation of the sphere, plotting the lines in a light gray color.

The plotting of latitude and longitude curves serves two purposes: it makes it obvious to the eye that we are plotting the globe, and it defines a surface upon which gnuplot can apply its `hidden3d` option, causing it to render a solid Earth. Without such a surface, we would be able to see through the globe and be confused by the drawing of the backs of the continents on the other side.

Making a labeled contour plot

We got an introduction to contour plots in *Chapter 8, The Third Dimension*, where we saw that the contours can be drawn in a sequence of dash-dot styles; the contour values can then be identified by referring to the legend that gnuplot constructs for us automatically.

There is another style of contour plot that incorporates numerical labels directly on the contours. gnuplot does not support this style directly, but can be tricked into compliance, as shown in the following figure:

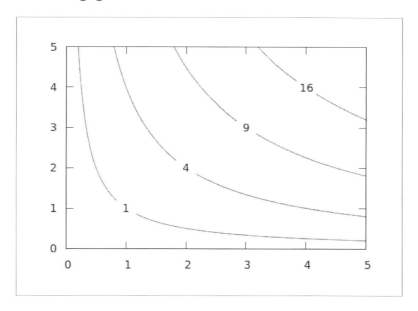

How to do it...

Type the following script:

```
unset key
unset surf
set view map
set contour base
unset clabel
```

```
set xrange [0:5]
set yrange [0:5]
set style fill solid
set for [n = 1:4] cntrparam levels discrete n**2
set for [n = 1:4] object n circle at n,n size 0.2 front fillcolor rgb
'#ffffff' lw 0
set for [n = 1:4] label n sprintf("%d", n**2) at n,n center front
splot x*y
```

How it works...

The first four lines set us up for making a typical contour plot (see *Chapter 8, The Third Dimension*). The command `unset clabel` turns off the automatic use of a sequence of colors or line styles for the contours; this will make all the contours the same color and style.

Our trick relies on defining a set of levels for the contours, and then setting the locations of some objects based on that set of levels and on the function that we are plotting. To do this conveniently, we use one of gnuplot's iteration commands (see *Chapter 7, Programming gnuplot and Dealing with Data*) three times. First, we set four `discrete` levels for the contours, which means we'll get four contours at those levels. We then define four circle objects that is, `circles` whose positions will lie on the contours. Two lines above this, the command `set style fill solid` will apply to the circles. Each circle has a size defined, is drawn in `front` of the other graph elements, is filled with white, and will have a zero border. The purpose of these circle objects is simply to obscure a section of each contour line to give a neater appearance and make the numerical labels easier to read.

The last iterative command defines four numerical labels. Each label has the same position as the corresponding circle, is drawn in front of everything, and has a text value encoded with the `sprintf` function using the code for an integer. What the label actually says is the same as the corresponding `cntrparam` value.

Softening the axes

The default gnuplot style gives roughly equal visual prominence to both the axes and tics and to the actual curves being plotted. Some may prefer the aesthetic properties of the style of plot illustrated in the following figure. In this graph, the curve is made to stand out by rendering the tics labels, border, and background grid in a lighter shade and using a thicker line for the curve:

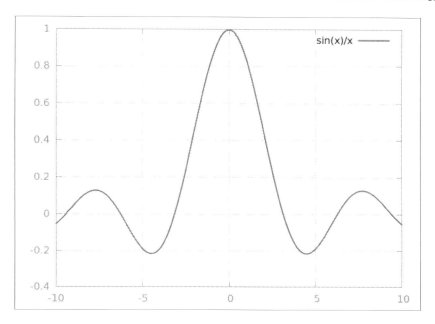

How to do it...

Load the following script into gnuplot to see the result:

```
set style line 2 lc rgb '#999999' lt 0 #grid
set style line 1 lc rgb '#999999' lt 1 #border
set grid linestyle 2
set border linestyle 1
plot sin(x)/x lw 2
```

How it works...

The set border and set grid commands accept a linestyle (see *Chapter 3, Applying Colors and Styles*). We've defined two styles, both with a mid-gray color. The linestyle for the grid will use linetype (lt) 0, which is dotted in most terminals, and that for the border will use linetype (lt) 1, which is solid. After defining these styles, we can use them in the set grid and set border commands, which we do in the following two lines. Finally, we specify a thicker linewidth (lw) in the plot command, and voilà.

Putting arrows on the axes

The following style is popular in the classroom:

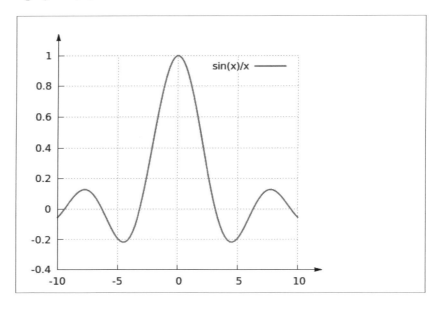

Notice that there is no border, but rather one pair of axes sporting arrows.

How to do it...

Execute the following script and you should see something very similar to the previous figure:

```
set arrow from graph 0,1 to graph 0,1.1 filled
set arrow from graph 1,0 to graph 1.1,0 filled
set tmargin 5
set rmargin 20
set border 3
set tics nomirror
set grid
plot sin(x)/x lw 2
```

How it works...

We learned about arrows in *Chapter 2, Annotating with Labels and Legends*. The first two lines define two arrows positioned using the `graph` coordinate system. This coordinate system is ideal for our purposes here, because `1` in this system is defined to be the very edge of the graph, which is exactly where we want the arrows to start. We also set them to be `filled`; as we saw in *Chapter 2, Annotating with Labels and Legends*, we can also, if we want, get very specific as to precisely how our little arrowheads are drawn. The `set border 3` command tells gnuplot to draw only a bottom and left border; type `help set border` for the full explanation of these numerical codes.

Plotting with pictures

A style, popular in journalism, for presenting a small set of data employs a technique illustrated in the following figure:

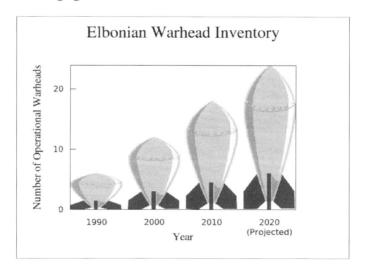

The previous figure shows the growth in warhead inventory of a fictional nation over time. A generic image of a bomb is scaled vertically to indicate the quantity for each year plotted.

Getting ready

The public domain bomb image that is used for the plot is called `bomb.png` and is provided in the datafiles folder for this chapter. You can modify this recipe to use your own pictures, in a variety of formats. To see which file types your version of gnuplot can use, type `show datafile binary filetypes` at the gnuplot interactive prompt. You will need to modify some of the parameters in the script to take into account the pixel dimensions of your image.

How to do it...

The following script produces the Elbonian bomb plot:

```
set title "Elbonian Warhead Inventory" font "Times,24" offset 0,2
set xlabel "Year" font "Times,12"
set xlabel "Year" font "Times,16"
set ylabel "Number of Operational Warheads\n" font "Times,16"
unset key
set tics nomirror
set xtics scale 0
set for [n = 0 : 3] ytics (sprintf("%d", n*10) 200*n)
set for [n = 0 : 3] xtics (sprintf("%d", 1990+10*n) 91+200*n)
set xtics add ("2020\n(Projected)" 691)
set cbrange [0:250]
set pal gray positive
set view map
unset colorbox
splot for [n = 0 : 3] 'bomb.png' binary filetype=auto\
center=(91+200*n, 300*0.2*(1+n), 0) dy=0.2*(1+n) with image
```

How it works...

The `offset` keyword in the first line pushes the title up by two character heights; without this we would find the title in the font we chose touching the border.

Our bomb image is 182 pixels wide by 600 pixels high. These numbers determine the values of some of the parameters in the remainder of the script. Our strategy will be to plot the image four times at different x-positions, each time with its pixels scaled differently in the y-direction. This will give the image a varying total height, determined by the scaling.

But first we must arrange our tics. We say `set xtics scale 0` because, although we want tic labels, we don't want tic marks on the x-axis. Following that command, there are two iterating `set` commands that use the syntax introduced in *Chapter 4, Controlling your Tics* to set the text and positions of four tic marks on the x- and y-axes. The actual range of the y-axis, for example, is from 0 to 600, because our bomb image is 600 pixels high. We use the `set ytics` command to place the values that we want to see in the proper places along the axis. We do the same thing for the x-axis, keeping in mind that our picture is 182 pixels wide. We are positioning tic labels at the centers of the images, which explains the use of the value 91 = 182/2. Finally, we replace the last x tic with one that indicates a "projected" year.

The `set cbrange` command sets the range of values mapped into colors in the palette. We have clipped this at the high end to render all values above the high limit as white. This has the effect of erasing the background around the bomb image. We've selected a grayscale palette and told gnuplot not to draw the color box, which is the legend that indicates how values are mapped to colors. This legend is useful for the kind of surface and image plots covered in *Chapter 8*, *The Third Dimension*, but here it conveys no useful information. Different palettes will create different color transformations of the image; it may be useful to experiment with these when producing a color graph.

The last line positions the input image four times on the graph. For typical image files, we need the keyword `binary`. The clause `filetype=auto` means that gnuplot will figure out that this is a PNG file from the file extension. For each iteration, we need to define the `center`, which is the (x, y, z) position of the center of the image, and we define a value for `dy`, which is the scaling for the y pixels and determines the height of the picture. Again, keep in mind the pixel dimensions of the image to see how this works.

Please note that, although this type of image plotting is discussed in the official documentation and in the online help, the information there is incomplete and in some places not correct.

Breaking an axis

Sometimes we would like to plot something over two disjoint domains, but want the plot to be contained in a single graph. In this case, we need to indicate that there is a discontinuity in the axis and generate two separate sets of tic marks, as shown in the following figure:

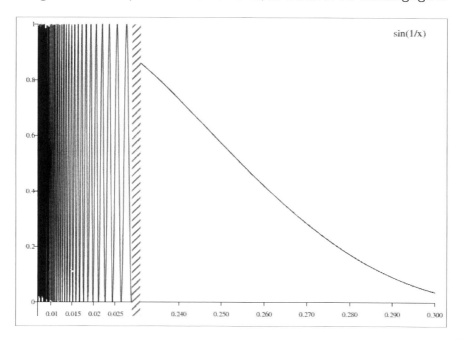

How to do it...

The following gnuplot script will produce the previous figure. It is provided with this book as a file called `breaking_an_axis.gnuplot`. Run it with **gnuplot breaking_an_axis.gnuplot** to get a PNG file that should look just like the previous figure. If you don't have the pngcairo terminal installed, you can use the png terminal or anything you wish, but you may get a different pattern in the vertical box. Type `test` at the gnuplot interactive prompt after setting your terminal (and output file if you are not using an interactive terminal) to see a list of the available patterns.

```
set term pngcairo font "Times,8"
set out "plot.png"
set border 2
set zeroaxis lt -1
set ytics axis nomirror
set xtics axis nomirror
set tics out
set samp 5000
set xrange [0.007:.1]
set yrange [-.05:1]
s = .2
b = 0.03
w = .001
h = 1
h(x) = sin(1/x)**2
f(x) = (x<b?h(x):NaN)
g(x) = (x>b?h(x+s):NaN)
set xtics .005, .005, .025
set for [n = 4 : 10] xtics add(sprintf("%.3f", s + n/100.0) n/100.0)
set object 1 polygon from first b-w,-h to b+w,-h to b+w,h to b-w,h to
b-w,-h front
set object 1 fillstyle pattern 5 lw 0
set key font "Times,12" samplen -1
plot f(x) title "sin(1/x)" lt -1, g(x) notitle lt -1
```

How it works...

The script plots a function over two disjoint sections of the x-axis; the first near $x = 0$ and the second from $x = 0.03$ to $x = 0.3$.

Setting up the axes

We include a font specification with the `set term` command to make sure there is enough space between the tic labels.

The command `set border 2` draws a border only on the left side of the plot, leaving the other three sides blank. `help set border` will explain the syntax.

The next command tells gnuplot to draw a pair of solid, black axes through the origin. We'll only see the *x*-axis, as the *y*-axis is off the graph. Its place is taken by the border.

The following three commands put tics on the axes and make them stick out of the graph area. We specify a large number of samples because our function is quickly varying and set an `xrange` to avoid the singularity at the origin. Our `yrange` leaves a little space below zero, which will allow our polygon to overlap the axis.

Defining the functions

Our goal is to plot the function `sin(1/x)**2` over two disjoint domains. To do this, we define three functions. But first, it is convenient to define a few variables. The variable `s` the *shift*, which is the amount by which the second segment of the graph is shifted relative to the first. We plot a piece of the function, then skip ahead by s along the *x*-axis, then continue. Next we define b, which is where the *break* occurs on the *x*-axis. The next two variables have only to do with the decoration that we shall use to indicate the discontinuity in x values: w is its width and h is its height, both in axis coordinates.

Now we define the functions. `h(x)` is simply the function that we are plotting. The next two are defined using the ternary syntax introduced in *Chapter 7, Programming gnuplot and Dealing with Data* where we learned how to plot on subintervals. `f(x)` is defined to be equal to our function `h(x)` below *x = b* (the breakpoint) and is set to be undefined above *x = b*. `g(x)` is defined to be `h(x)` but shifted by an amount s, and is only defined above the breakpoint.

Setting up the tics

We need two sets of tics and tic labels for the two separate sections of the plot.

The tics for the left-hand section are defined with the line `set xtics .005, .005, .025`: the syntax is *start, interval, end*.

The tics for the right-hand section are established with the following line, which uses gnuplot's looping syntax (see *Chapter 7, Programming gnuplot and Dealing with Data*). For each value of *n* in (4, 5, ... 10), we add a tic at position *n*/100. The label printed for the tic is encoded using the `sprintf` function, which uses the same syntax as in the C language. `%.3f` means to represent the number as a float with three decimal places. The numbers that we print are shifted by the shift variable s. Since we are shifting the tics and the function argument by the same amount, the graph will be correct.

Indicating the break

We need some device to show that there is a discontinuity in the set of x coordinates. Here we've chosen a style that makes this hard to miss, by creating a long, thin rectangle enclosing a hatch pattern that lies over the break in the axis.

To do this, we use gnuplot's new `object` facility. We define a `polygon` object using the variables that we defined earlier for its width and height, and for the breakpoint. The final point repeats the first to close the polygon.

The next line sets some properties of the polygon. We set its fill pattern and set its linewidth (`lw`) to zero so it won't have an outline.

And finally...

Before plotting, we want to make the legend font bigger, since we set the default font a little small to make room for the tics. The clause `samplen -1` causes the legend to be printed with no line sample, since there is only one curve. Thus, we're using the key as a convenient way to make a title for the plot that will save space by being placed inside it.

The plot command in the last line plots both segments of the curve as black solid lines (`lt -1`), sets the title for the curve, and makes sure not to repeat the title for the second part.

Fitting the grid to the data

gnuplot, by default, arranges our graph with a set of ticmarks at equally spaced intervals, with gridlines to match (if we turn the grid on). If we want to make it easy to read off the values of a particular set of points, we can do better:

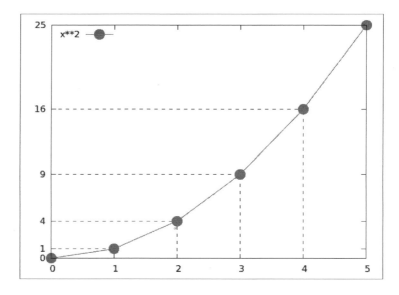

How to do it...

The following script will create the previous figure:

```
set term pngcairo dashed
set out 'xsquared.png'
set samples 6
set key top left
set for [n = 1 : 4] arrow from first n, 0 to first n, n**2 back \
    nohead lt 7
set for [n = 1 : 4] arrow from first 0, n**2 to first n, n**2 back \
    nohead lt 7
set for [n = 0 : 5] ytics (n**2)
plot [0:5] x**2 with linespoints pt 7 ps 3
```

How it works...

We have included explicit `set terminal` and `set out` commands because we want our linetype specifications to select a dashed line; if you prefer to use colored lines where the figure has a dashed line, you can omit the `dashed` keyword.

We set a small number of samples because we want to illustrate the technique with a handful of points, that typically might be read from a datafile.

After placing the legend in the top-left corner where it will not collide with the data, we use iteration to define two sets of four arrows. The coordinates of their starting and ending positions are taken from the positions of the tic marks and the function that we plan to plot. The keyword `back` puts the arrows behind the data points, and `lt` (linetype) 7 is the desired dash style for our simulated grid (this will vary with terminal). We don't want arrowheads. These sets of arrows will simply take the place of the automatic grid that gnuplot would otherwise draw for us, which would not intersect the data points.

The next iterative command sets the `ytics` to align with the six plotted points.

Finally, we plot the function, choosing the pointtype (`pt`) that maps to a solid circle in this terminal, and a fairly large pointsize (`ps`).

Coloring the axes

We showed back in *Chapter 1, Plotting Curves, Boxes, Points, and more,* how to use two different *y*-axes when plotting two functions or datasets that have dissimilar ranges. We can make it easier to see which curve goes with which axis by using color.

In the following figure, two curves are colored (shaded in print) to match corresponding colors on the vertical axes with which they are associated. The axis labels are colored to match, as well. This makes it easy to match the curves with their *y*-axes without having to use arrows or legends.

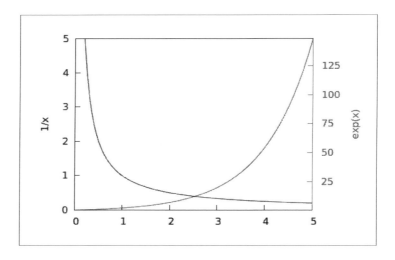

How to do it...

The following script created the previous figure:

```
set multi
set tmargin at screen .8
set rmargin at screen .8
set lmargin at screen .2
set bmargin at screen .2
unset key
set tics nomirror
set xrange [0:5]
set border 8
set border lt 4
set y2tics 0,25,150
unset ytics
set y2label "exp(x)" textcolor lt 4
plot exp(x) axis x1y2 lt 4
set border 7
set border lt -1
set ylabel "1/x" textcolor lt -1
unset y2label
```

```
set ytics 0,1,5
set tics nomirror
unset y2tics
set yrange [0:5]
plot 1/x lt -1
unset multi
```

How it works...

There are several ways to cajole gnuplot into yielding this effect. We've chosen to use **multiplot** mode to draw two different graphs and arrange to have them precisely overlaid.

The first line enters multiplot mode. When drawing a set of graphs in multiplot mode that need to be aligned on top of each other, we need to set global margins in screen coordinates. That's the purpose of the four margin commands.

We then have some familiar range and tic setting commands for the first plot, and a `set border` command that tells gnuplot to draw the right vertical border only. We've also set the linetype (`lt`) of the border to yield a light magenta, which should appear as gray in print. We want the tics and labels to appear on the right (y2) axis only, and our plot command selects the same linetype as was used in the border. So we have one curve plotted against an axis with the same color. The command for setting the `y2label` contains the clause `textcolor lt 4`, which will cause the label to be drawn in the same color as is used for linetype 4; so the curve, axis, and axis label describing the curve are all in the same color.

For the second plot, which will be associated with the left-hand *y*-axis, we `set border 7`, which draws a bottom, left, and top border (type `help border` to see how this works). We select a solid black linestyle (`lt -1`) for this part of the border, and the same linetype for plotting the curve and defining the `ylabel`. The commands for unsetting the unused tics and preventing mirroring need to be repeated as in the script to prevent extra, unwanted tic marks and labels.

The technique of overlaying plots in multiplot mode by setting screen margins only works for fairly recent versions of gnuplot, but can be used for many advanced plotting techniques, such as aligning a contour plot and a 2D plot of a cross-section of the contours.

Finding Help and Information

I hope that this book has been useful to you in getting gnuplot to do what you need it to do. But no single book can contain everything you might need to know. So, in this Appendix, I have compiled a brief list of other sources of gnuplot information and education.

The most direct and immediate source of help when using gnuplot is the built-in help system; by typing the `Help` *topic* at the interactive prompt you can get detailed information on any topic. This is most useful if you already have some idea about what you are looking for. Sometimes the help system provides too much information, and often not enough, but this is usually the first place to look if you need to know all the options associated with a particular command.

The official gnuplot manual, which can be found in various HTML and PDF configurations at the official gnuplot home at `http://gnuplot.info/documentation.html`, contains some detailed information that cannot be found anywhere else, and is an essential reference work for the advanced gnuplotter. Beware that it is impossible to actually learn how to use gnuplot from this manual, however, and it is organized in a way that makes it difficult to find relevant information.

There is a gnuplot reference card at `http://www.gnuplot.info/docs_4.0/gpcard.pdf`, which is a brief reminder of the most useful commands and options, suitable for printing out and tacking up next to your computer.

There is a great collection of gnuplot demos indexed from `http://gnuplot.info/screenshots/index.html#demos`.

More beautiful 3D sample plots (with scripts) can be found at `http://ayapin.film.s.dendai.ac.jp/~matuda/Gnuplot/pm3d.html`.

The first book treating gnuplot in detail was *Gnuplot in Action* by Philipp K. Janert, which can be found at `http://www.manning.com/janert/`. This is more concerned with teaching data analysis than gnuplot *per se*, but is a well-regarded volume.

The page of gnuplot tips and "not so Frequently Asked Questions" by T. Kawano at `http://t16web.lanl.gov/Kawano/gnuplot/index-e.html` has some very useful information and examples, although it was last updated in 2005.

More gnuplot demonstrations can be found at `http://www.csse.uwa.edu.au/programming/gnuplot_demos/`.

An impressive collection of *Gnuplot tricks*, showing some nonobvious ways of doing things with gnuplot, can be discovered at `http://gnuplot-tricks.blogspot.com/`.

David MacKay's lovely examples of using gnuplot in physics can be found at `http://www.inference.phy.cam.ac.uk/teaching/comput/C++/examples/gnuplot/index.shtml`.

The involved subject of date/time plotting in gnuplot is given a tutorial treatment by Marco Fioretti in the article *How to handle time-based data with Gnuplot* at `http://www.zdnetasia.com/how-to-handle-time-based-data-with-gnuplot-62301350.htm`.

The gnuplot mailing list is archived at `http://news.gmane.org/gmane.comp.graphics.gnuplot.user`, and the newsgroup `comp.graphics.apps.gnuplot` can be scanned at `http://groups.google.com/group/comp.graphics.apps.gnuplot/topics`. You should keep an eye on both of these if you want to keep up-to-date; gnuplot is actively developed.

Finally, I maintain a page about gnuplot at `http://lee-phillips.org/gnuplot`. Its original purpose was to help people who want to install gnuplot on the Macintosh, but now serves up general information and maintains a current list of links to other gnuplot resources. You will also be able to find updated and, if necessary corrected code and data files for use in this book, on this page.

Index

V

vector plot
  about 147
  creating 148
view 137
Vim 164
volatile data
  handling 132
Volatile Data Source 132
volatile keyword 133

W

Web
  interactive plot, creating for 114, 115
webGUI
  writing, fot gnuplot 168-173

web page
  plot, including in 112, 114
whiskerbars 28
world.dat datafile 181
wxt terminal 96

X

xlabel command 37
xrange 90

Y

ylabel command 37

Z

ztics value 137

Thank you for buying
gnuplot Cookbook

About Packt Publishing

Packt, pronounced 'packed', published its first book "*Mastering phpMyAdmin for Effective MySQL Management*" in April 2004 and subsequently continued to specialize in publishing highly focused books on specific technologies and solutions.

Our books and publications share the experiences of your fellow IT professionals in adapting and customizing today's systems, applications, and frameworks. Our solution based books give you the knowledge and power to customize the software and technologies you're using to get the job done. Packt books are more specific and less general than the IT books you have seen in the past. Our unique business model allows us to bring you more focused information, giving you more of what you need to know, and less of what you don't.

Packt is a modern, yet unique publishing company, which focuses on producing quality, cutting-edge books for communities of developers, administrators, and newbies alike. For more information, please visit our website: www.packtpub.com.

About Packt Open Source

In 2010, Packt launched two new brands, Packt Open Source and Packt Enterprise, in order to continue its focus on specialization. This book is part of the Packt Open Source brand, home to books published on software built around Open Source licences, and offering information to anybody from advanced developers to budding web designers. The Open Source brand also runs Packt's Open Source Royalty Scheme, by which Packt gives a royalty to each Open Source project about whose software a book is sold.

Writing for Packt

We welcome all inquiries from people who are interested in authoring. Book proposals should be sent to author@packtpub.com. If your book idea is still at an early stage and you would like to discuss it first before writing a formal book proposal, contact us; one of our commissioning editors will get in touch with you.

We're not just looking for published authors; if you have strong technical skills but no writing experience, our experienced editors can help you develop a writing career, or simply get some additional reward for your expertise.

Matplotlib for Python Developers

ISBN: 978-1-847197-90-0   Paperback: 308 pages

Build remarkable publication quality plots the easy way

1. Create high quality 2D plots by using Matplotlib productively

2. Incremental introduction to Matplotlib, from the ground up to advanced levels

3. Embed Matplotlib in GTK+, Qt, and wxWidgets applications as well as web sites to utilize them in Python applications

4. Deploy Matplotlib in web applications and expose it on the Web using popular web frameworks such as Pylons and Django

NumPy 1.5 Beginner's Guide

ISBN: 978-1-84951-530-6   Paperback: 234 pages

An action-packed guide for the easy-to-use, high performance, Python based free open source NumPy mathematical library using real-world examples

1. The first and only book that truly explores NumPy practically

2. Perform high performance calculations with clean and efficient NumPy code

3. Analyze large data sets with statistical functions

Please check **www.PacktPub.com** for information on our titles

LaTeX Beginner's Guide

ISBN: 978-1-84719-986-7   Paperback: 336 pages

Create high-quality and professional-looking texts, articles, and books for business and science using LaTeX

1. Use LaTeX's powerful features to produce professionally designed texts

2. Install LaTeX; download, set up, and use additional styles, templates, and tools

3. Typeset math formulas and scientific expressions to the highest standards

4. Include graphics and work with figures and tables

GNU Octave Beginner's Guide

ISBN: 978-1-84951-332-6   Paperback: 280 pages

Become a proficient Octave user by learning this high-level scientific numerical tool from the ground up

1. The easiest way to use GNU Octave's power and flexibility for data analysis

2. Work with GNU Octave's interpreter – declare and control mathematical objects like vectors and matrices

3. Rationalize your scripts and control program flow

4. Extend GNU Octave and implement your own functionality

Please check **www.PacktPub.com** for information on our titles

3329888R00120

Printed in Great Britain
by Amazon.co.uk, Ltd.,
Marston Gate.